Two Families

Two Families

TREATIES AND GOVERNMENT

Harold Johnson

PURICH
PUBLISHING
LIMITED
SASKATOON, SK. CANADA

Purich Publishing Ltd.
Box 23032, Market Mall Post Office, Saskatoon, SK, Canada, S7J 5H3
Phone: (306) 373-5311 Fax: (306) 373-5315 Email: purich@sasktel.net
Website: www.purichpublishing.com

Library and Archives Canada Cataloguing in Publication

Johnson, Harold, 1957-
    Two families : treaties and government / Harold Johnson.

ISBN 978-1-895830-29-3

    1. Cree Indians – Saskatchewan – Treaties. 2. Cree Indians – Saskatchewan – Government relations. 3. Indians of North America – Canada – Treaties. 4. Indians of North America – Canada Government relations. 5. Whites – Canada – Relations with Indians. 6. Cree Indians – Saskatchewan – History. 7. Cree Indians – Legal status, laws, etc. – Saskatchewan. I. Title.

Cover design by Duncan Campbell.
Cover photograph by Bob Michayluik Photography; Treaty Medal courtesy Office of the Treaty Commissioner, Saskatchewan.
Editing, design, layout, and map by Donald Ward.
Printed in Canada by Houghton Boston Printers & Lithographers.

Publisher's Note: Some legal case citations are to CanLII (www.canlii.org), a not-for-profit organization initiated by the Federation of Law Societies of Canada, which provides free access to legal resources.

URLs for websites contained in this book are accurate to the time of writing.

The publishers gratefully acknowledge the assistance of the Government of Canada through the Canada Book Fund and the Government of Saskatchewan through the Saskatchewan Arts Board's Grants to Publishers program.

Printed on 100 per cent post-consumer, recycled, ancient-forest-friendly paper.

This book was written at the behest of a student and is dedicated to all students, whether in an academic institution or in the study of life.

To my wife Joan, my children Michael, Harmony, Ray, Anangons, and Memegwams.

To my grandchildren Ethan, Gus, Liz, Hayden, and Nevaeh.

In memory of my mother, her mother, and her grandmother.

Treaty No. 6 (1876) and Adhesion (1889)

CONTENTS

MONTREAL LAKE CREE NATION

BOX 106
MONTREAL LAKE, SASKATCHEWAN
S0J 1Y0
TELEPHONE: (306) 663-5349   FAX: (306) 663-5320

December 12, 2006.

To: Kiciwamanawak,

     As Chief of the Montreal Lake Cree Nation, I endorse the writing of Harold Johnson. His use of the inclusive "Kiciwamanawak" in the discussion formally introduces him as the speaker for all of us to all of you. If he were to use Niciwamak, he would be speaking only for himself to all of you. As the elected leader of the day, I personally endorse his words on behalf of his people.

Sincerely,

Chief Lionel Bird
Montreal Lake Cree Nation

OFFICE OF THE CHIEF

Kiciwamanawak

Matri.... Surrounding

I AM HAROLD JOHNSON. My mother's name was Mary, my grandmother's name was Catherine, my great grandmother's name was Elizabeth. I know the stories of Elizabeth's mother and father and how he took Elizabeth's mother as his third wife, but I do not know their names.

This is the proper way to introduce myself — not only to tell you my name, but to tell you my lineage through my mother so that you know how I came to be here. I am of this land. I am of this earth. I live at the place where my grandfather, Redmond Bradfield, moved his family after they were kicked out of the territory that became Prince Albert National Park. I live 200 metres from where the adhesion to Treaty No. 6 was negotiated and agreed upon in 1889. This adhesion added roughly 11,066 square miles of territory to Treaty No. 6. A hundred metres from here is a cemetery where my relatives are buried.

I do not speak for all Aboriginal peoples. I do not have that right. I speak only for myself, for my ancestors for seven generations behind me who prepared the way for me, and for my children and grandchildren and great grandchildren and ... seven generations ahead.

I spea[k] Setting :from Saskachewan hical centre of Saskatchewan. He[re is where ...] Here is where my mother told me the stories of my ancestors, and the stories of my great-grandfather, James Ross. It is the stories about this man that have informed my understanding of the relationship between Indians and Whites, and this understanding has shaped my life and my work.

James Ross was present at the signing of the adhesion to Treaty No. 6. Throughout his life, he refused to purchase a hunting, fishing, or trapping license (his sons bought and carried a license for him). He believed that the government did not have the right to interfere in how he made a living. The day would come, he often warned, when we would need a licence to go *misi* in the woods. He refused to live on a reserve, and spent his life travelling the territory. He lived where he wanted and moved when he felt the need. His final residence is a rectangular mound a little way down the lake from where I now live.

Fish taken from Crean Lake, SK, 1931. Crean Lake was known as Big Trout Lake prior to the formation of Prince Albert National Park. My mother was born here Dec. 4, 1921. The photo was taken a year after all the Aboriginal people living within the boundaries of the park were forced to leave. (Glenbow Archives, na-3229-71.)

My mother's grandparents, James and Elizabeth, and the stories they told shaped my mother's life, as she, in turn, shaped mine. This land holds those stories. They are in the trees and the moss, in the water, in the animals, and in the air. They can help us to live here in a good way if we learn to listen.

It is not the tradition of my people to preach. We understand that things work out better if we wait until we are asked before we share what we have learned. This book would not have been written were it not for a law student who once asked me about treaties. After I explained my understanding, he asked me to write a book so that he would have a source to quote when he was writing papers. This book is for him and for other students, studying law or any other discipline, and for people who are studying life, whether they are in an academic institution or not.

This book is not meant solely for academics, so I have chosen to write it the way I would sa_____ Everything I say comes from the understanding of _____ace of lakes, rivers, and boreal forest. _____ where my ancestors are buried, where their atoms are carried up by insects to become part of the forest, where the animals eat the plants in the forest, and where my ancestors' atoms are in the animals that I eat, in my turn. I am a part of this place. I do not say that I own this land; rather, the land owns me.

Kiciwamanawak, my cousin: that is what my Elders said to call you. When your family came here and asked to live with us on this territory, we agreed. We adopted you in a ceremony that your family and mine call treaty. In Cree law, the treaties were adoptions of one nation by another. At Treaty No. 6 the Cree adopted the Queen and her children. We became relatives. My Elders advise that I should call you my cousin, *Kiciwamanawak,* and respect your right to be here.

You are my relative under the law of my people, and I have some things to say to you. I do not mean to interfere in your life, and I do not mean to tell you what to do. But take what I say and use it in a good way, if you can; if you cannot use it in a good way, you should leave it here.

It is not my intention to make you feel badly about what has happened between our families. There is nothing you or I can do to change the past.

(handwritten note: reason why book was written)

People made choices and we live with the consequences. They were not our choices. There is nothing we should feel badly about.

What I am saying here is not to criticize or to lay blame. That would not help anyone. Instead, *Kiciwamanawak,* I want to explain to you who we are, the First Nations and our laws. I want to tell you our history and show you how it differs from what you might have been told. I will talk about law, yours and mine, and how they coexist under the Creator's law. I will show you how your supreme law, the *Constitution,* fits into our supreme law, and how they are consistent with each other. Then I will suggest how we might live together as two families sharing the same territory. I will never suggest that you go back where you came from, for I assure you, *Kiciwamanawak,* that you have a treaty right to be here.

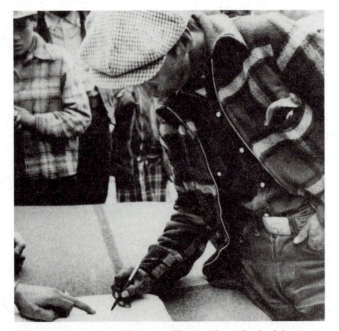

Ocheise man signing adhesion to Treaty No. 6, Rocky Mountain House, AB, 1950. (Glenbow Archives, na-1954-6.)

CHAPTER ONE

My Family

WE ARE THE FIRST NATIONS OF THIS TERRITORY. Our genesis stories tell of our creation here. These stories differ from what you may have been told. We did not walk across the Bering Strait, as some people suggest. The Bering Strait theory began with the writings of Jose de Acosta (1540-1600), a Jesuit who has been described as the Pliny of the New World. In 1590, Acosta published *The Naturall and Morall Historie of the East and West Indies*, in which he relied on the Bible to prove that the Indians came from the Garden of Eden and must have walked across a land bridge in order to have come to the Americas. Translated into English in 1604, the theory was developed further by scientists after Darwin speculated that the earth had been in existence for longer than a literal interpretation of the Bible would allow. But religion continued to play a part in the theory; some speculated that the Indians were the lost tribes of Israel.

The Bering Strait theory preserves the biblical accounts of creation and provides a justification for the dispossession of Indian lands, making First Nation peoples simply previous immigrants. As Rena Dennison has written:

One of the most accepted ideas of the academic world is commonly called the Bering Strait Theory. It is taught as an absolute fact in many textbooks and has been, it seems, zealously guarded by many in the academic community. The accepted idea is that Native people first migrated here 12,000 years ago from across the Bering Strait, and then spread through what is now North America and South America in a somewhat orderly and methodical migration. New evidence has raised a great many questions about this cherished theory. There seem to be more than 500 sites scattered from Pennsylvania to Chile that date in the neighbourhood of 40,000 years of age. One site may well be around 47,000 years of age and is located in north-eastern Brazil.[1]

Our genesis stories tell us that we have been here since our Creator created us. We have lived on our Mother the Earth for all of our time. This relationship between our Creator, our Mother, all other life forms, and ourselves forms the basis of all that we know to be true. This relationship forms the basis of our law.

Our families were here when your family arrived. We were not starving. Our lives were not "nasty, brutish, and short," as Chief Justice Allen McEachern suggested in his 1991 judgement in *Delgamuukw* v. *British Columbia*:

> [I]t would not be accurate to assume that even pre-contact existence in the territory was in the least bit idyllic. The plaintiff's ancestors had no written language, no horses or wheeled vehicles, slavery and starvation was [sic] not uncommon, wars with neighbouring peoples were common, and there is no doubt, to quote Hobbes, that aboriginal life in the territory was, at best, "nasty, brutish and short."[2]

We lived through the stages of life, from infancy to our coming-of-age ceremonies to our adult years. As parents, then as grandparents, we fulfilled our duties, and finally, as elders, we died and went back to the earth. We were well provided for. "Everywhere we looked there were our food and our medicine," as Elder Alma Kytwayhat has said.[3]

Your historians, *Kiciwamanawak*, knew of our good health. In 1670, Virgil J. Vogel wrote:

Skeletal remains of unquestionably precolumbian date . . . are, barring a few exceptions, remarkably free from disease. Whole important scourges [affecting Europeans during the colonial period] were wholly unknown. . . . There was no plague, cholera, typhus, smallpox or measles. Cancer was rare, and even fractures were infrequent. . . . There were, apparently, no nevi [skin tumours]. There were no troubles with the feet, such as fallen arches. And judging from later acquired knowledge, there was a much greater scarcity than in the white population of . . . most mental disorders, and of other serious conditions.[4]

Two years later, in 1672, Nicholas Denys observed that Aboriginal people "were not subject to the gout, gravel, fevers or rheumatism. The general remedy was to make themselves sweat, which they did every month and even oftener."[5]

In 1908, historian George Wharton James wrote:

Before the Indian began to use the white man's foods, he was perforce compelled to live on a comparatively simple diet. His choice was limited, his cooking simple. Yet he lived in perfect health and strength . . . and attained a vigour, a robustness, that puts to shame the strength and power of civilized man.[6]

My family's oral histories tell of a time of plenty and of magic. People were able to talk to the animals and perform miracles. We were not "simple, childlike people," as Christopher Columbus reported.[7] Columbus was unable to understand people who lived without deceit.

We lived in a society that was different from yours. Our societies could be described in terms of ecology. That is a good word, "ecology." It is the best word in your language to describe the complexities of our society. Ecology describes the relationships of species within a territory, and how those species interact symbiotically. The observations made by ecologists over the past 100 years or so parallel the observations of my ancestors over the course of millennia. I am not saying that we lived according to your science of ecology; all I am saying is that the scientific concept of ecology is a useful analogy of how we lived and understood the environment. There was nothing artificial, rigid, or tyrannical about our societies. We lived according to the laws of the Creator, which incidentally look a lot like the laws of ecological order.

Kiciwamanawak, your law is not superior to the law of the Creator. Your law is quite simple, by comparison. Lawyers, judges, and law professors create the illusion of complexity for their personal gratification and benefit. Under the law of the Creator, students try to simplify things to understand the intricacies of multiple relationships. Under the law of the Creator, a student can spend a lifetime trying to understand three words:

Beatrice Olson (née Brown) and a little girl on Nemeiban Lake, SK, circa 1957– 58. Beatrice attended residential school with my mother. Beatrice was older and took my mother under her protection. She continued to trap well into her 80s, and was known to walk 40 miles to her trapline. (James Brady. Glenbow Archives, pa-2218-880.)

"All My Relations." This phrase is said at the end of a prayer, but it is also said whenever we take something from nature. It is used to signify when a person is finished speaking, and it is a prayer in itself. But who are my relations? How should I relate to them? Why should I remember them when I gather from nature? Why should I remember them when I finish speaking? There are simple answers to these questions, but no complete ones. I could spend a lifetime trying to understand, and never know it all. Under the law of the Creator, there are no professors, no experts. No one presumes to know it all; we are all forever students. If a person suggests that he knows something completely, it is a sure sign that he has stopped learning.

"Our canoeman for three days." My Great Uncle Adolphus Ross, with Christina Bateman and Annie McKay, on their way to La Ronge, 1919. Adolphus often wore a suit jacket, as here. When I knew him, he was bent with age, but he continued to wear a jacket, shirt, dress pants, and mocassins. When western medicine was unavailable, people from our area sought assistance from Adolphus, who had an understanding of traditional medicine. (Saskatchewan Archives, S-B510.)

Under the law of the Creator, it seems that the more a person learns, the more a person develops his understanding, the more humble he becomes. Humility develops when a person understands enough to realize that he knows very little. The closer a person comes to understanding the totality of a system, the more she realizes how little she really understands.

Our elders are not experts. They are senior students. They know they are human and fallible. That is why they tend to be careful when they give advice, and that is why their advice is dependable. Isn't it better to receive advice from someone who has learned enough to realize the enormity of the question than from people who arrogantly believe they know something?

Many of our elders have been to the edge of the abyss of understanding. They know more than someone who has only seen it from afar. When something is seen from a distance, it appears small, and some people are fooled into believing that they have an understanding of it.

The anthropologists who have studied my family have made only a rudimentary sketch of our social organization. They have viewed us from your perspective, and from a distance. One of their purposes seems to have been to justify your culture of domination. Traditionally, my family members have viewed every assumption of superiority by your family as a sign that you knew nothing. They assumed that, with time and patience, your family would develop in its understanding and you would give up this misguided notion.

We are equals, *Kiciwamanawak*. Our forms of social organization are equally appropriate. Our families are both made up of real people. This territory we share is capable of supporting all of us in health and happiness. We should be living as two families in the same territory. When your family arrived in the southern part of this territory, there were several families already co-existing here. The Nehiyaw, the Dakota, the Anishinabae, and the Métis families had worked out between them how they would live together under the Creator's law. None of these families either exercised or expected to exercise authority over the others.

When your family arrived here, *Kiciwamanawak*, we expected that you would join the families already here, and, in time, learn to live like us. No one thought you would try to take everything for yourselves, and that we would have to beg for leftovers. We thought we would live as before, and that you would share your technology with us. We thought that maybe, if you watched how we lived, you might learn how to live in balance in this territory. The treaties that gave your family the right to occupy this territory were also an opportunity for you to learn how to live in this territory.

Adolphus Ross and William Bird, 1919. This photograph was taken at the site of the negotiation and signing of the 1889 adhesion to Treaty No. 6, where the Montreal River begins. My cabin is located about 100 metres downstream from this spot, which was likely a natural camping or stop-over area. (Saskatchewan Archives, S-B513.)

Duncan Bird, second Chief of the Montreal Lake Cree Nation, in his treaty jacket. Bird signed the adhesion to Treaty No. 6 in 1899 as a band councillor. (Montreal Lake Cree Nation.)

CHAPTER TWO

Your Family

KICIWAMANAWAK, YOUR COURTS, POLITICIANS, AND PHILOSOPHERS have never been able to articulate a coherent theory of your sovereignty in this territory without relying on the out-moded doctrine that you have a right to this territory because you are superior to my family. Without a coherent theory based on equality, we are left to assume that you rely on ideals similar to those held by the Ku Klux Klan and the Aryan Nations. What else can we assume but that you are white supremacists?

Yet, as your own courts have ruled, your ancestors' "discovery" of us gave you no automatic rights over us.[8] If it had been otherwise, if we had "discovered" you, our laws would not apply to you, even if we thought you were living in tyranny and wanted to save you from self-destruction. Our law of non-interference, choice, respect, and responsibility would have prevented us from imposing our law on your ancestors. Even in International Law, which is your family's law applied to the whole planet, discovery does not provide justification for occupation. Discovery cannot be justification for your family's occupation of this territory. Your family did not discover this place. It was never lost.

Christopher Columbus, on his first voyage, wrote:

Sir: Since I know that you will be pleased at the great victory with which Our Lord has crowned my voyage, I write this to you, from which you will learn how in thirty-three days I passed from the Canary Islands to the Indies, with the fleet which the most illustrious king and queen, our sovereigns, gave to me. There I found very many islands, filled with people innumerable, and of them all I have taken possession for their highnesses, by proclamation made and with the royal standard unfurled, and no opposition was offered to me.[9]

Indeed, Pliny's *Natural History* relates how some of my relatives were blown by a storm to the shores of Germany in the last century B.C.E.[10] So, according to your own history, we "discovered" you one and a half millennia before you "discovered" us.

Neither did your ancestors conquer mine. "Put simply," as one of your courts ruled in 2004, "Canada's Aboriginal peoples were here when Europeans came, and were never conquered."[11] Happily, we have had no wars between us in this territory, and I pray we never do.

"When we look back to the past, we do not see where the Cree Nation has ever watered the ground with the white man's blood," Tee-tee-quay-say said to the Treaty Commissioner. "He has always been our friend and we his."[12]

Your relatives to the south, in the territory called the United States of America, used conquest as a justification for their occupation of the territory of the Aboriginal peoples. The rest of the world has largely ignored this, although, according to your own International Law, it is illegal; conquest does not justify occupation.

The idea of *terra nullius* — an expression from Roman law meaning that the land was empty, unoccupied, or uncultivated[13] — was used by your relatives to colonize Australia, though that, too, has now been put to rest in International Law[14] and largely abandoned by Australia's highest court.[15] In Canada, however, the idea that my family had no right to the territory they occupied and that the land was therefore open for the taking has persisted. Duncan Campbell Scott, the poet who became Superintendent of Indian Affairs, wrote in 1914 that "the Indian in himself had no title to the soil demanding recognition, nor, in his inferior position as a savage, had any rights which could become the subject of Treaty or negotiation."[16]

Scott's conclusions have been discredited — he was a product of his time and his Empire — and modern thinkers have come to the opposite conclusion: that the only right you have to occupy this territory must come from treaty. You have a treaty right to occupy this territory. The only coherent theory that provides for your sovereignty that is not based on supremacist ideology is that you obtained the right to be here through negotiation and agreement. Your rights to take and use the natural resources abundant in this territory, and your rights to enjoy the bounty of the earth, were given to your family by mine at treaty. All your wealth has come from the earth, whether it was trees, grazing land, or nutrient-rich soil, or minerals, oil, and gas, or granite for your buildings. The treaties gave you access to the wealth you now enjoy.

And what wealth you have acquired, *Kiciwamanawak*. You live in one of the richest nations on the planet. The world recognizes that the opportunity to live in this territory is equivalent to winning a lottery. Your family in Canada makes up less than half of one percent of the population of the world. Your accumulation of material goods, your hoarding of resources, your consumption of the earth's bounty, puts you in a position in which the rest of the world either envies or despises you.

You were given the right to live here and enjoy the benefits of the land, but you were not given the right to waste, pollute, and destroy. My ancestors could not give you that right because they did not have it themselves, and you cannot give away what is not yours.

The Supreme Court has agonized over Aboriginal and treaty rights, and, in case after case, has concluded that your family should treat my family better.[17] The judges have repeatedly said that, when the government is dealing with my family, the honour of the Crown is at stake. Then those same judges make rulings that assert your family's sovereignty over my family without giving a coherent explanation of how your family acquired it. We are left to assume that the Crown stole sovereignty, and that certainly is not honourable.

The only coherent theory of your family's acquisition of sovereignty in this territory is that my family gave it to you at treaty. Your sovereignty is a treaty right. There are many areas in Canada where your family does not have treaties with my relatives. I do not speak for them. I only urge you, as your own courts have urged you, to begin negotiations with those people before you make plans to remove the natural resources from those unshared territories.

Honourable Alexander Morris, Lieutenant-Governor of Manitoba, the North-West Territories (later Saskatchewan and Alberta) and Keewatin (1872-77); negotiator on behalf of Her Majesty Queen Victoria at Treaties No. 3 through 6. (From Story of Manitoba, *Vol. 1; Glenbow Archives, na-3242-1.)*

CHAPTER THREE

The Adoption of Your Family By My Family

WHEN YOUR ANCESTORS CAME to this territory, *Kiciwamanawak*, our law applied. When your ancestors asked to share this territory, it was in accordance with our law that my ancestors entered into an agreement with them. It was by the law of the Creator that they had the authority to enter treaty.

The Creator gave us several ceremonies through which we experience, learn, and practice the law of the Creator. One of these ceremonies is for adoption. While your law is divided into several areas — tort, property, criminal, contract, taxation — our law is primarily concerned with the maintenance of harmonious relations. Despite its seeming simplicity, the complexity of the Creator's law makes it impossible for a human being to learn all of it in a lifetime. The best we can hope to achieve is a single drop in the river of understanding.

It was in accordance with the law of adoption that my family took your ancestors as relatives. We solemnized the adoption with a sacred pipe. The promises that my ancestors made are forever, because they were made under the Creator's law. This adoption ceremony is what we refer to when we talk about the treaty.

Alexander Morris (1826-1889) was appointed the Queen's Commissioner to negotiate treaties with my family. He was the Lieutenant-Governor of Manitoba and the North-West Territories. During his term of office, he negotiated Treaties No. 3 through No. 6 with the First Nations of Western Canada. In regard to Treaty No. 6, he wrote:

> The Treaties made at Forts Carlton and Pitt in the year 1876 were of a very important character. The great region covered by them, abutting on the areas included in Treaties Number Three and Four, embracing an area of approximately 120,000 square miles, contains a vast extent of fertile territory and is the home of the Cree nation.[18]

On behalf of your family, Morris gave my family commemorative medals at Treaty No. 6. These medals have, on one side, an image of Queen Victoria, and, on the other, the images of a White man and an Indian with their hands clasped. Other symbols include the sun, the grass, a tipi, and a hatchet with the blade buried in the ground. The symbolism is obvious: your family and mine were to be equal. We were to be brothers and sisters for as long as the sun shines and the grass grows. The buried hatchet indicates perpetual peace between us. The tipi represents our continued traditions and way of life. Central to the symbolism is the brother-to-brother relationship.

Treaty Medal used for Treaties No. 3 through 8. (Bob Michayluik Photography; Medal courtesy Office of the Treaty Commissioner, Saskatchewan.)

Alexander Morris represented your Queen in the ceremony of treaty. He used the promise, "as long as the Sun shines, the Grass grows and the River flows,"[19] as an indication of how long the treaty would last. Morris knew the importance of the words, if not their precise meaning. We understand that there are spiritual aspects to the sun, the grass, and the river (water), and if promises are made that invoke these spirits, then the maker of the promise and all his descendants are bound by that promise. A promise made to these spirits cannot be broken. If a mere human tries to break such a sacred promise, those spiritual forces will interfere to ensure the promise is kept. The negative consequences of their interference are borne by those who attempt to break the promises made in their names.

Your family designates billions of dollars annually toward my family. The Department of Indian and Northern Affairs oversees this spending. You spend $70,000 per year to keep just one of my relatives in prison. Your professionals in justice, health, education, and social services scratch their heads and wonder why things keep getting worse, and ask for more money. I suggest that, if you were to keep the promises made at treaty, the costs to you, and to us, would be far less. It is far more costly to your family, in terms of money, effort, and frustration, to keep on trying to renege on the treaty promises than if your family would accept and abide by the terms it agreed to.

The treaties are forever. We cannot change them because the promises were made, not just between your family and mine, but between your family and mine and the Creator. There were three parties at the treaty. When my family adopted your family, we became relatives, and that cannot be undone. A bond far stronger than any contractual obligation holds us together. Your law of contract and treaty allows for breach and remedy. The Creator's law does not allow for any breach whatsoever. Failure to comply has consequences, and no matter how severe the failure, the promise never becomes null and void; the consequences just keep getting greater and greater.

The treaties in this territory were made with the Queen. She is the one we adopted. She and her children received the right to occupy this territory alongside my family. She sent her representative to ask permission for her children to farm here.

Remember, at that time the buffalo were disappearing. Many of my family had recently died of diseases for which we had no medicine. I am not angry with you, *Kiciwamanawak*. I am not angry that the buffalo were slaughtered, or that the Northwest Mounted Police chased the last herds into the United States to deny my family access to food. I am not angry that small pox and influenza carried by Europeans killed so many of my family. Holding this anger in is not easy, and I am helped by the memory that my ancestors at treaty were not angry. They did not point to the Queen's representative and say, "You killed the buffalo, so now you must feed us." Instead, my ancestors showed compassion and adopted your family.

We expected that you would behave like relatives and help us in hard times, just as we took the responsibility to help you if you needed it. We expected to keep living as a family with a new family in the neighbourhood. We were happy the new family had technology and would share it with us.

We accepted that the buffalo would no longer supply us with food, clothing, shelter, tools, and medicine. We accepted the offer of technology transfer, and it was written into the treaties that we would receive farm equipment and instruction. We were happy that our children would receive education, and that you would share your medicine with us.

We were especially happy when the Queen's representative indicated that he understood our persistence in claiming that we did not want to be interfered with in our hunting, fishing, gathering, and trapping across the shared territory. He said:

> Understand me, I do not want to interfere with your hunting and fishing. I want you to pursue it through the country, as you have heretofore done; but I would like your children to be able to find food for themselves and their children that come after them.[20]

If the Queen's representative understood this, then it would seem that he understood how our families would share this territory. Hunting, fishing, gathering, and trapping are our way of being on this earth. It is how we relate to our Mother and her provision for us. It is integral to our relationship with all living things. We are related to the animal nations and the plant nations as surely as we are related to you.

The adoption at treaty of your family by my mine held promise of a good future for our children. Seven generations ago my ancestors prayed for me, as I pray seven generations ahead. Our law is not only ancient; it is modern and forward-looking. You became my relative at treaty, you are my relative today, and our children and grandchildren and great-grandchildren, and so on, will be relatives in the future. We have an obligation, *Kiciwamanawak,* you and I, to make things right between us so that the future generations do not inherit our missed opportunity.

When we adopted your family, we asked that you stop selling alcohol. My ancestors made the Queen's representative aware of the destruction alcohol caused to our family.[21] I have read your history books that say the Northwest Mounted Police came into this territory to protect us from American whisky traders. These books do not talk about the whisky sold by the Hudson's Bay Company and the Northwest Company. I suspect the Northwest Mounted Police came here to protect your family's traders from competition, because whisky sales have never stopped in this territory.

Today, the biggest bootlegger in this territory is the provincial government. Not only does it profit from the suffering of my family, it subsidizes alcohol sales. In the northern communities where freight costs raise the price of milk, for example, to twice that charged in the southern cities, the price of alcohol sold in provincially run stores is exactly the same as it is in the cities. This same provincial government took action against the tobacco companies because it perceived that tobacco was affecting your health. Yet, the government sells alcohol to us, without putting warnings on the bottles that consumption by pregnant women will result in our children being born with fetal alcohol syndrome. *Kiciwamanawak,* I understand that your ancestors to the south brought slaves from Africa to the Americas to work in sugar plantations. These people had a life expectancy of only a few years owing to the harshness of the conditions under which they worked. The sugar they produced was used to make alcohol that was used, in turn, in trade with my family. Your family used the same strategy with opium in China. Your family is skilled at exploiting the weaknesses of your trading partners.

I have a hard time holding back my anger when I think of my nephews' and nieces' needless suffering and the extreme profit made on that suffering. It must be my sadness that holds back the anger — my sadness when

I think of my brothers and sisters frozen to death, mangled in car crashes, knifed, shot, and beaten. Did you know, *Kiciwamanawak,* that most of the people in your prisons were impaired when they committed the crimes that resulted in their incarceration? Did you know that many of the people in your prisons are suffering from greater or lesser degrees of fetal alcohol syndrome? When we consider that the provincial government provided the alcohol in the first place, the prisons that are full of my brothers and sisters begin to look like a plot.

Elders have told me that the men who designed the prisons and those who run them are extremely smart. These elders perceive how the treaty promises of education and the promise to be good neighbours have been subverted, for the help and education we receive come in the form of a prison sentence. In prison we are fed and sheltered and get a hard education.

I am not going to say that you intended prisons as a means of fulfilling your treaty obligations. But now that you know, every day that it continues I can impute intention to you, *Kiciwamanawak.* If you know that this is happening and do nothing about it, then you must intend it to continue. But if you and I do not stop this tragedy from continuing, *Kiciwamanawak,* our children — yours and mine — are going to inherit both the suffering and the costs.

We agreed to share medicine with each other at treaty. The Queen's representative promised a medicine chest. Many modern pharmaceuticals are derived from Aboriginal knowledge. There are stories of your people seeking out our Medicine People on the pretext of a malady to obtain our medicine, then going back to their laboratories and synthesizing the active ingredient — for profit.

There is enough medicine for everyone. All our needs are provided for by the Earth our Mother. There is no health care crisis. The problem is not a shortage of medicine, or a shortage of trained people. The problem is a shortage of generosity. The problem is greed. Your doctors have seized the highest level of the health care system, an artificial structure dominated by the College of Physicians and Surgeons, whose chief purpose is to maintain the elevated status of doctors. The College of Physicians and Surgeons regulates itself with the support of your law. It is against your law to practice medicine without a licence. By limiting the number of licences, the people in the college create a shortage of doctors; the same is true, to a lesser extent, of nurses and technicians. The artificial shortages allow these people to demand higher and higher salaries, but that's not the problem. The problem is that, ultimately, people are denied the health care they have become dependent on.

Other people in the health care system advise the sick, the aged, and the crippled that there is no money to help them. But the sick, the aged, and the crippled are not asking for money; they are asking for help. The problem is that they are asking for help from people inside a closed system, people who benefit from keeping the system closed.

I appreciate that my analysis appears over-simplified. Many will argue that health care is a complex issue that requires complex analysis and inquiry. We can continue to add layers and layers of complexity, if we choose. We can analyze drug patents and economic factors and labour issues and provincial and federal jurisdictions with all the concomitant legal complications, or we can simply assert that good health is the most important factor in our existence, and the law must mend itself to achieve that outcome. A simple principle, a starting point, can cut through the layers of complexity.

CHAPTER FOUR

Your Family's Justice System

THE PRIMARY FUNCTION of the provincial Law Society is to maintain the high costs of legal assistance. It is against your law to practice law without a licence, and the licence holders whose economic interests can only be protected by limiting the number of licences available determine the distribution of licences.

I am a lawyer. I am a parasite. I live on the suffering of others. I am compelled to abide by the rules of the Law Society or face disbarment. To effect change, I must participate in the very system that oppresses me and my family.

In this territory, prior to your family's occupation, my family members took care of each other. We had few episodes of anomie — social instability or alienation caused by the erosion of moral and social codes — because people belonged and participated. In every community in this territory where a police force was instituted, community control has collapsed. The old rules of behaviour no longer apply, and many of my family are compelled to rely upon your family's inadequate justice system. My family's social structures have been shattered by generations of residential schools, missionaries, social workers, churches, resource officers, police, resource extraction corporations, and their concomitant trade unions.

Your family has imposed institutional order upon my family. The problem is more obvious among the youth. Many have completely lost an understanding of our traditions. They do not know how to be Indian. At the same time, they do not accept your traditions. They do not assimilate. They do not respect either tradition, and therefore find themselves in conflict with both my family and yours. When they behave without respect, one of my family phones the police. The reason we phone the police is because we no longer have our own structures to handle anomie or imbalance. Your family has imposed its own traditions and structures on us, and now my family has become dependent on them. We desire the peace and security common to our heritage, and when it is disrupted we phone the police because we do not have the power to deal with it ourselves. One document I examined showed that the RCMP had been called to a single residence in Northern Saskatchewan over 50 times in a three-month period.

Your family's justice system has not brought order to my family. Rather, it has displaced the order that was there with one that is both foreign and inadequate. The more a community is destroyed by the imposition of an unworkable system, the more likely the incidents of anomie. The imposition of your justice system on my family is not a solution to crime; it has become the cause of crime.

A high percentage of "crimes" dealt with in the provincial courts are system-generated offences. Breach of probation, failure to appear, breach of recognizance: these are crimes only in the face of an egotistical court. A breach of probation is not necessarily an expression of disrespect for the judge who imposed the order. Often the probation order is simply impossible to comply with. It usually requires the probationer to reside at a prescribed residence and not consume alcohol. But the order does not ban other persons at that residence from consuming alcohol. The order usually requires the probationer to keep the peace and be of good behaviour, but it does not require the probationer's relatives and friends to keep the peace. When everyone in the house is drinking and losing control, the probationer is compelled by curfew to remain in the residence. Probationers are expected to adhere to an unreasonable standard and then compelled to live in conditions that subvert that standard. Because our communities have been devastated, because we experience extreme rates of anomie in some areas, because our power to correct has been usurped, probation requires my relatives to live by rules that are impossible to follow.

System-generated offences choke the provincial courts. Judges and prosecutors become agitated at my relatives who have long criminal records, but usually the record is an accumulation of system-generated offences. Peter is charged with assault and given one year probation. While on probation he gets in another fight. Someone phones the police. Peter now has another assault charge on his record, as well as breach of probation. The judge imposes a period of probation twice as long as before and sends Peter back into the same environment. The judge wants to teach Peter to respect the courts.

My family understands respect. Respect is the basis of our understanding. Traditional teachings inform us that, in order to receive respect, we must first be respectful. Respect cannot be demanded; it must be earned. No one can be forced to respect. Force only produces resistance. Tyranny is despised. Only when your justice system learns to respect my family will members of my family begin to respect your justice system.

No one is impressed with the suits and ties and robes, the reams of paper and the occasional Latin phrase except the people wearing the suits, the ties, and the robes, wasting paper and blathering ancient terminology. To my relatives in handcuffs and shackles, the self-aggrandizement of the participants in the judicial process does not instil confidence. It simply serves to alienate further. The victims of the courts are rarely impressed by the education and brilliance of the lawyers and judges.

The people who run law schools do not pretend that a legal education prepares students for the practice of law. Their function is to act as the door to the profession. The regime of study is excessively rigorous, and purposely so. Law school is made difficult to keep out the undesirables, and for no other practical reason. The regime of study is best suited to male, Anglo-Saxon students with adequate financial resources. I know of young women whose menstrual cycles were affected by the stress of law school. I personally experienced periods of emotional confusion where I surged between joy and despair brought about by the stress of examinations, and I am not a person easily stressed.

Your law is not complex, *Kiciwamanawak*. When compared with ecology, it is very simple. Most of your law is written in legislation. The law not written in legislation — the Common Law — comes from tradition and previous judges' decisions. Your law is available for anyone to read, and anyone brought up with your values will have little difficulty in understanding it. Lawyers, judges, legislators, and especially law professors, like to make the law appear complicated. It suits their sense of personal importance and feeds their economic advantage.

Kiciwamanawak, you and I cannot afford to allow these people to interpret our treaty.

In the early time in your law, a person could prove the truth in two ways: by ordeal or by combat. If the accused chose to prove the truth by ordeal, he had two choices: by water or by fire.[22] If he chose water, he was bound and thrown into a lake or river. If he sank, the water was deemed to have "received him" and he was fished out. God had favoured him, legally, though often he drowned in the process. If the accused chose ordeal by fire, a red-hot piece of iron was placed in his hand and the hand was bound.

Big Bear and Poundmaker, signatories to Treaty No. 6. The photograph was taken while both men were incarcerated in Stony Mountain Penitentiary (1886). (Hall and Lowe, Winnipeg; Glenbow Archives, na-1315-18.)

Three days later the hand was unbound. If the hand was infected, it was accepted that God had not favoured this person because he had not told the truth. At that time, infection likely led to death.

The other way to prove the truth was by combat. Again, it was accepted that God intervened on the side of the truthful. The untruthful died.

Trial by ordeal faded away, but trial by combat continued with the addition of the use of champions to do combat for the accused.[23] Trial by battle was only removed by legislation in 1818.[24] The last time trial by combat was attempted was in 1985 when a defendant in the High Court of Judiciary in Scotland unsuccessfully challenged the lord advocate, claiming that the 1818 statute only applied in England.[25] If a person was speaking the truth, it was accepted that God would favour his champion in combat. These champions became the first lawyers.

Law has not changed much since then. Today, lawyers do combat for their clients with words and style. The truth is often lost while lawyers exhibit their knowledge, strutting in finery and speaking in riddles. Judges and juries, and the occasional reporter, determine the winner of the battle based more often on the presentation of the lawyers than on a comprehensive assessment of the facts. Courtroom drama, made popular by television, is exactly that: a stage performance by actors disconnected from reality and emotion, except where emotion is part of the act.

The adversarial system of law, born out of mortal combat, cannot resolve conflict. We cannot kill the differences between us by fighting each other. We have to join together to kill our differences.

Your family tells stories about my family: that we fought a multitude of wars among ourselves, and that our entire existence was premised on war. In 1823, the American Chief Justice John Marshall wrote:

> But the tribes of Indians inhabiting this country were fierce savages, whose occupation was war, and whose subsistence was drawn chiefly from the forest. To leave them in possession of their country was to leave the country a wilderness; to govern them as distinct people was impossible, because they were as brave and high spirited as they were fierce, and were ready to repel by arms every attempt on their independence.[26]

This presumption underlies American jurisprudence with regard to Aboriginal peoples. The presumption is false. We did not kill each other in our interactions. If we had anything like war between us, it was about killing the differences between us more than it was about killing each other. It was more important to show bravery than it was to kill. It is said that the Cree and Dene were enemies, but the stories tell us more often about tricks we played on the Dene than about killing. I am certain the Dene tell stories about how they outsmarted the Cree.

Kiciwamanawak, there are many differences between your family and mine. But if we come together with good minds and healthy spirits, we can heal the differences. If we let ourselves get caught up in the adversarial process, we will remain adversaries forever.

A judge's decision, even a Supreme Court decision, does not resolve differences. In the adversarial system, there are always winners and losers. The loser who is forced to live with the decision rarely walks away without vowing retaliation. When my family wins a case in your courts, the bureaucrats invariably implement only the minimal condition of the ruling. We have known for a long time that, whenever we make legal advances by means of and through your justice system, we can expect a backlash. Likewise, when we are denied a right, we return home and assert the right in other ways.

Our constant battling in your courts does not put our families on the same road into the future. You have a treaty right to occupy this territory, *Kiciwamanawak.* We should be working together to defend our treaty. The conflict that the people in the justice system exaggerate and perpetuate comes from misunderstanding. To end the conflict, you and I must learn to understand each other.

CHAPTER FIVE

Reconciliation of Laws

THE MISUNDERSTANDING OF MY ANCESTORS at treaty was linguistic and conceptual. We did not understand your language or your concepts of property. When Commissioner Alexander Morris explained the written terms of the treaty through an interpreter, my ancestors likely did not understand the underlying concepts that would be familiar to your family. It is not certain that he did explain all the terms of the written text. His journals and letters do not indicate that he explained the meaning your family associates with the words "cede, release, surrender and yield up . . . all rights, titles and privileges."

Our oral histories do not indicate that we agreed to separate ourselves from our Mother the Earth, but they are consistent with our understanding of our role as humans under the laws of the Creator, which mandates that we should be kind and generous and share the bounty of the earth with each other, with the animal nations, the plant nations, and with you, *Kiciwamanawak*.

The misunderstanding between us, *Kiciwamanawak*, is the difference between the written text of the treaty and our oral histories. If we go to the original paper the treaties are written on, the first thing we notice is that large parts of it were pre-written, with spaces left for the Treaty Commissioner to fill in. These spaces that are filled in include our names and which articles of agricultural equipment would be supplied. The important terms about our relationship with our Mother the Earth were pre-written. Can you, *Kiciwamanawak,* in good conscience, insist upon these terms that were likely not mentioned and, even if they were, not likely understood, and were definitely not negotiated?

The Commissioner's oral promises were different from the written text of the treaties. For example, at Fort Pitt he said:

> I see the Queen's councillors taking the Indian by the hand saying we are brothers, we will lift you up, we will teach you, if you will learn, the cunning of the white man. All along that road I see Indians gathering, I see gardens growing and houses building; I see them receiving money from the Queen's Commissioners to purchase clothing for their children; at the same time I see them enjoying their hunting and fishing as before, I see them retaining their old mode of living with the Queen's Gift in addition.[27]

The text of the treaty states:

> ... the said Indians, shall have the right to pursue their avocations of hunting and fishing throughout the tract surrendered as herein before described, subject to such regulations as may from time to time be made by her Government of her Dominion of Canada, and saving and excepting such tracts as may from time to time be required or taken up for settlement, mining, lumbering or other purposes. . . .

Tustukeeskuais, one of the Cree chiefs who signed treaty at Fort Pitt, was reported as saying after the provisions of the Sacred Promise had been explained to him and others at Fort Pitt: "I am glad that all my friends and children will not be in want for food hereafter. I am glad that we have everything which we had before still extended to us."[28]

I doubt the Treaty Commissioner explained the treaty in a way that conveyed the meaning the Crown assigned to the words, "cede, release, surrender and yield up ... all rights titles and privileges," and the limits to be placed on hunting and fishing. If the meaning of these words had been conveyed, it is doubtful that Tustukeeskuais would have been pleased to learn that hunting and fishing were to be regulated, and that he would be confined to a reserve.

Elders familiar with the oral histories dispute the written record of the treaties. The people who wrote the record did so from their perspective and understanding. When the written record is compared with the oral history, it is clear that much of what my family members said to the commissioner has been omitted, and that which has been recorded has been perverted.

Some of the discrepancies might be explained by errors in translation. Others might be explained by the lack of understanding of our customs, traditions, and worldview. But cultural arrogance on the part of the recorder is likely the greatest factor. The problem with the written histories is that we are now left with the perspective of a single individual who followed his own view of what was important and what was not when he chose what to include and what to omit. The original purpose of recording the discussions was to have something to report back to your government. It is apparent that those who recorded the proceedings sought to impress their superiors by writing a version that showed the commissioner and his party in the best light.

Oral history does not suffer from this flaw. The oral historian is bound by the internal consistencies of our language and by the law of conse-

Treaty with Saskatchewan Cree at Fort Carlton, SK, 1881.
(From Canadian Illustrated News, *Dec. 16, 1876; Glenbow Archives, na-1406-177.)*

quence. Oral historians know in their deepest core that if they misconstrue, add, or delete, then they, their children, and their children after them will suffer the negative consequences of it.

I suspect your reliance on the authority of written records comes in part from the stories of Moses and the tablets of stone on which were written the Ten Commandments (Exodus 34:28). Our stories tell us that the Creator wrote the law in our hearts. The laws that Moses brought down from the mountain are good laws, but they were written not on the hearts of humans but on stone. The difference between oral history and the written record begins with our different conceptions of God and the law. The Ten Commandments, written in stone, are authoritative. They represent the will and the word of God.

But for the vast majority of your history, few people could read and write. Until recently, the Bible could only be read by priests, who cloaked themselves with the authority of God. The written word of God then became the authority of men, who inserted themselves between you and God. The written text of God's word was presented to you not so much as the authority of God but as the authority of men who could read.

By keeping the ability to read and write to themselves and presenting the written text as absolute authority, these men created the first artificial shortage. Your society was designed by men who created artificial shortages. Today, you experience a shortage of money to the benefit of bankers, a shortage of good health to the benefit of doctors, a shortage of justice to the benefit of lawyers, and a shortage of God to the benefit of priests. These artificial shortages have all been created by men of higher learning who claim that their education makes them superior. They draw their authority from their textbooks, and never mention that the shortage of education was artificially created for their benefit.

The authority of the written text has been presented to you as justification for the authority of men of position and letters for so long that everything written has become accepted as truth. Only now that more people can read for themselves is the written text beginning to be challenged. With vast numbers of the world's population still unable to read, it will be a long time before the truth of the written text is laid bare. But I assure you,

Kiciwamanawak, it will be laid bare. Humankind refuses to remain illiterate. Your systems are being challenged the world over.

The written text of the treaties has no more authority than the oral histories. The authority assigned to the written text is a subversion of what really happened. Remember, your ancestors asked to share this territory. My family agreed to share it, in accordance with our laws, our traditions, and our understanding of the ecological order that is part of the great mystery of creation. We were the holders and the keepers of this territory. It is by our law that the treaties should be interpreted, because our law was the first law of this territory. Your family came under our law when you came to this territory. This is simple. You abide by the laws, customs, and traditions of the people in whose territory you reside. This is a principle of your law as well; thus, the saying, "When in Rome, do as the Romans do."

Our laws are not to be interpreted according to Western European legal principles. The men and women who act as judges in your Supreme Court have tried to understand the position of First Nations in Canada. They have tried to imagine a place for us within your social structure. The problem is that our law does not adapt itself to artificial, hierarchical structures. Our law, written in the hearts of humans, is the law of equality. Our law cannot abide the subjugation of the many by the few. The artificial shortages that seem essential to your social organization are contrary to our law, which mandates that everyone should have equal access to the gifts and generosity of the Creator and our Mother the Earth.

Our law does not adapt to abstractions. It is the law of every day, of every human. It is not the law of fantasy and imagination. It will not allow humans to imagine themselves in boxes and believe that the boxes are natural and necessary. Under our law, no person should allow another to come between himself and the Creator, and no person should assume to come between another and the Creator. Your hierarchies tend to come between humans and their source of equality. In your earlier time, priests assumed the authority of intermediaries between the masses and God, which gave them an elevated status. Likewise, monarchs assumed authority by the principle of the divine right of kings. They ruled because they declared themselves God's anointed. The divine right of kings is based on the 13th-century notion of the monarchy as sacramental. As God's anointed, the monarch ruled by the will of God, not by the will of Parliament or the people. The rest of your hierarchies, based on artificial shortages, come between the masses and the bounty of the earth.

When your ancestors signed treaty, *Kiciwamanawak*, you were freed from the tyranny of artificial shortages. You came under the law of equality.

The law of the Creator is pragmatic. We use it to walk in the everyday world in a good way. The law of the Creator does not support abstract structures. There is no Canada, really. You are people who inhabit a certain territory, and some of you assume positions within government, in justice, in education, and labour. But Canada is only people inhabiting a portion of Creation. Beyond that, our law does not extend. You can agree, among yourselves, that some people will have status and authority, but you cannot surrender your responsibilities to an abstract concept like government. You cannot blame government for anything. You can try to blame the people to whom you surrendered your authority, but ultimately it is your own fault

Anglo-Rouyn Mines, north of La Ronge, SK, 1956. The mine became feasible when the government of Saskatchewan built a road connecting La Ronge with Flin Flon, MB, where the Hudson's Bay Mining and Smelting Co. had facilities to refine the ore. (James Brady; Glenbow Archives, pa-2218-826.)

for giving away your authority in the first place. You cannot blame General Motors, IBM, or the Hudson's Bay Company. They do not exist. There are only presidents, vice presidents, secretaries, and labourers that deny individual responsibility based on abstract concepts of limited liability.

Your law allows abstract concepts and grants personal status to nothingness. Behind the shelter of the law, enormous injustices are committed not only against my family but against the poor of every family, who are forced to sell their labour as resource extractors of one sort or another.

Under our law, everyone has a right to the bounty of the earth: to the food she provides, to the medicines, to shelter, to clothing. All our physical needs are provided for, and the resources are there for everyone. Artificial entities such as Imperial Oil cannot have a greater right than humans to the resources of the earth. This is a territory rich in resources, abundant with timber, water, minerals, medicine, fruit, vegetables, wildlife, and fertile soil for cultivation. Everything we need for a good life is here. It is only because of the laws of property, and the fact that property can be held by artificial entities that create shortages for profit, that people in this territory go hungry, or do not own their own homes.

Most of the resources of this territory are extracted in exchange for inadequate salaries and then exported, with the bulk of the wealth accumulating in the coffers of people who manipulate artificial entities. Your family builds highways that run primarily north and south to carry the wealth of this territory away. Popular economic theory holds that a nation that exports more than it imports is a wealthy nation. But think about it: if you export all your resources, you will eventually become poor. If we imagine wealth as cash, then we are momentarily wealthier, but if we imagine wealth as access to resources, then in the long run, exportation must lead to poverty.

You have a treaty right to this wealth, *Kiciwamanawak*. Why is my family denied access to the bounty of the earth while people hiding behind artificial entities accumulate more than their fair share? It is only by your law that these people justify their acquisitiveness. Under our law, no one has a greater right than anyone else. We are all entitled to health and happiness. This law was in existence when your ancestors first asked to share this territory with us. The treaties are based on this law. Your right under treaty to occupy this territory flows from this law.

It would be presumptuous of us to try to enforce the law of the Creator. The Creator's law is to be learned. It requires that we learn to walk in balance and to understand balance: balance between men and women, between families, between us and the plant and animal nations. This moment is a balance between the past and the future. All things were put here in balance with everything else. When our relations with others go out of balance, there is anomie, and there are negative consequences as balance reasserts itself.

Today, when a family gets out of balance, the authority of the state is invoked and a social worker is empowered to remove the children, who are then placed in foster homes or institutions. After a childhood spent bouncing back and forth among the state apparatus of social workers, psychologists, juvenile courts, and institutions, these children achieve the age of majority, and then no one wants to invoke the state any more as justification for interference. When this legal adult, who has never experienced balance, and does not even know any of his relations, commits a crime, the state is invoked again to send the offender to a correctional facility. Prisons cannot teach people to live in balance, for everyone there, including the guards, are out of balance.

The word "balance" and "ecology" are good words in your language to explain the principles of my family's understanding of our relationship with, and hence the law of, this territory. These words do not encompass the entire principle, but they are sufficient for the purposes of this discussion. Balance requires a lifetime of learning. Life itself is a balance with death. The individual will only survive if he learns to find his place in the balance of family, community, nation, and environment.

Your law tends to confuse balance with conflict. In the adversarial system of your courts, balance means the manipulation of the relative power of adversaries. Thus, rules are created to ensure a fair contest. Defence and prosecution, plaintiff and defendant are cast in roles that are limited by rules, not to achieve equilibrium but to prolong the conflict. The rules of your courts keep the parties fighting. Judgement is not a solution; rather, it is the simple declaration of a winner and a loser. Solutions require the balance of family, community, nation, and environment.

Even in those areas of the law where balance should be foremost, such as in family law, your legal system tends to deny the existence of relationships, imposing contractual obligations instead. The human relationship is too complex for the court system to cope with, so a legal fiction is created whereby such relationships are reduced to contracts. Thus, marriage and divorce are reduced to contracts. Humanity is written out of the system.

The treaties between us were negotiated on behalf of your Queen. We assumed she was a real person, the head of a large family, and that she had honour. Artificial entities have no emotion, no spirit, no honour. The state cannot show kindness and pity. Even the written texts of treaty make it clear that the treaties were between people, not artificial entities. Treaty No. 6 states:

> And whereas the said Indians have been notified and informed, by her Majesty's said Commissioners, that it is the desire of Her Majesty to open up for settlement, immigration, and such other purposes as to Her Majesty may seem meet, a tract of country bounded and described as hereinafter mentioned: and to obtain the consent thereto of Her Indian subjects inhabiting the said tract; and to make a Treaty and arrange with them so that there may be peace and good will between them and Her Majesty, and that they may know and be assured of what allowance they are to count upon and receive from Her Majesty's bounty and benevolence.[29]

When the state is invoked, real people deny responsibility. It becomes too easy to say, "The state is sending you to prison," "The state is taking your children," "The state doesn't want you to hunt here." The bounty and benevolence of the Queen, promised at treaty, are those things that can normally be expected from a relative, someone taken in adoption, and their family.

We did not adopt an artificial entity; our law does not recognize them. We adopted the Queen and her children: real people, people with spirits, people capable of experiencing and showing kindness and pity. Artificial entities such as the state cannot learn to live in balance. They are incapable of experiencing sorrow, and hence kindness and pity. The state cannot *experience*. It has no life to learn from, no heart to look to for understanding. When the state is invoked by real people, these people deny what life and experience should have taught them. They deny kindness and pity, and withhold the bounty and benevolence of the Queen Mother.

It is not for me to tell you how to live. It is not for me to say how you arrange your family, how you govern yourselves. I cannot tell you what to do. I am a human, the same as you, and, as such, I am capable of making mistakes. It is not for me to tell you what to believe or not to believe. If you want to believe in artificial entities, that is up to you. But I can only relate to you as one human to another, one relative to another. *Kiciwamanawak*, I experience you as a person and want you to experience me as a person rather than a subject.

And yet, I have hope. I recently spoke with a provincial court judge. I was gently teasing him about Provincial Court Judges asking for a salary increase to $200,000 per year. He said he was embarrassed by it. In his court, there is a prosecutor, a defence attorney, himself, and a clerk. Each of them could move over one chair and accomplish the same task. Therefore, they should all be paid the same.

Retired Chief Judge Barry Stuart from the Territorial Court of Yukon wrote in his decision sentencing Marcellus Norman Jacob:

> Yet in the wind are more than just whispers of change coming from every direction. Some within the justice system embrace the changes, some oppose them. For me, Marcel Jacob pushed me over the edge. He was born and grew up on my watch.
>
> No one I know within the justice system would have knowingly participated in the steps that produced Marcel's behaviour. We all did. We all did because we pay too much homage to the system.[30]

Judge Stuart showed us that he was a human and took responsibility and did not hide behind the system and his robes. Judge Gerry Morin of the Saskatchewan Provincial (Cree) Court pushes the envelope of practice and procedure in his court every day to find justice. Judge Mary Ellen Turpel-Lafond looks for solutions that work in her court. She has tried to make a difference for people who appear before her suffering from fetal alcohol syndrome. These are real human beings who take responsibility and deal with the most out-of-balance people in our communities. These judges work within the most elaborate and artificial system ever designed by the minds of men and look to their hearts for guidance.

These people are at the pinnacle of your justice system as my relatives experience it. Provincial courts determine much of our lives, far more than appellate courts or the Supreme Court of Canada. The experience of real men and women dealing with everyday people gives these judges the expertise that I would like to see used to interpret the treaties when they come into your courts.

Your family tends to see things in opposites. Your discussions are a dichotomy: thesis and antithesis. Yours is a language of opposites: good and evil, anger and joy, heaven and hell, right and wrong, truth and deceit, light and dark, generosity and greed, pride and humility, envy and munificence.

Your *Indian Act* once outlawed my family's ceremonies because you believed we were practicing evil, a contradiction of the Judeo-Christian tradition in which you were raised. But this accusation as a justification for supremacy ignores the wrongs done in your own family. In trying to formulate an ideology based on polarity, you necessarily ignore all the other possible solutions.

Kiciwamanawak, not everyone believes that humankind is innately evil and only through salvation can see the Creator. In my family's understanding, we are to walk in balance. Good and evil are the extremes that we avoid. We see a vast array of ways of being between these extremes. Our way of being is our understanding of where we are in relation to our environment. This understanding has many more possibilities than the extremes of good and evil.

Good and evil are but parts of the whole. My family understands that ecology has order, that everything around us is part of the whole. Thoughts and dreams and prayers have substance within that whole. An out-of-balance thought can cause disruptions within the whole, just as an out-of-balance action can. If we were to define evil according to my family's understanding, the closest we might come would be a lack of balance. We do not see evil everywhere. All we see are the Creator's blessings, the bounty of Mother Earth, and people making choices.

I have never met an evil person, *Kiciwamanawak*. I have met many that are so out of balance as to be a danger to themselves or others. But I have never met a truly evil person. Even after all that my family has endured these last centuries, I cannot honestly accuse you or your family of evil.

In this pivotal moment, *Kiciwamanawak*, there are extremes of wealth and poverty in our territory. Some do not have enough to meet their needs, while others have far more than they will require in their lifetime. In this pivotal moment, *Kiciwamanawak*, there are people in prison who do not belong there. There are people who are hungry, people who are sick, people who have given up hope and languish in despair. We have to make a choice in this moment, to do something — anything — or do nothing. Whatever our choice, it will permeate the great mystery and return to us. The consequences are neither good nor evil; they just *are*, and we will have to live with them.

This territory can provide for all our physical needs and the needs of many others. But it cannot provide for all our wants, for our wants exceed our needs. If we can learn to live in balance in this territory, we can expect long, healthy, and happy lives. It is our choice.

Your family has had a huge impact on my family in the past few centuries. But when we examine your family, we find that my family, likewise, has had a huge impact on yours. We have affected your structures to the extent that your needy family members are now treated as poorly as ours. Your justice system is harsh, and the same treatment is now meted out upon members of both our families who are poor and without resources.

Since the first contact between our families, we have affected each other. The wealth that flowed from Turtle Island, where Columbus first landed, has significantly shaped your political landscape. Your merchant classes were once counted among the lower orders in your society. New wealth increased their influence and, over centuries, eventually toppled monarchies and considerably reduced the influence of the church. The merchant class demanded freedoms similar to those that had been granted the barons who forced King John to sign Magna Carta in 1215. Your version of democracy is, in part, a result of those demands. International law underwent massive changes as new theories were required to legitimize the transfer of wealth from the colonized to the colonizer. Your family's health improved with imported foods. Your population increased as you found new medicines. Your home territory became the wealthiest in the world, and the wealth came from elsewhere in the world.

We are related, *Kiciwamanawak*. Whatever you do to me will have consequences for you. We are bound by the law of adoption. We cannot ignore that law. As long as you insist on your doctrine of superiority, you will be in breach of that law, and you will not develop your understanding.

There are several areas where my family and yours are involved in discussions. You will be outside those discussions as long as you insist on dominating them. It seems that when we hold talks, my family is only allowed to speak when your family likes what we are saying. Often, people in your government agencies will undermine my family's contribution. When my family asserts its understanding, your policy analysts insist that it be restated in terms of their own structural requirements. Only when we fill in the proper forms, only when we conform to the rules of your structures, only when we prostrate ourselves to your structures and your superiority is our voice allowed to be heard. By your requirement that we speak only in the language of structure, you exclude yourself from the discussion that occurs between my family and everyone who does not belong in your family.

Today we are in a world far different from that of our forefathers. We have connectivity. There exists a global communications system wherein my family and others carry on discussion — not dialogue, which is between two, but a discussion, which is among many. For the past two decades my family and other Aboriginal families have carried on discussions within the United Nations, where my family has voice. Our voice combines with other Aboriginal families' voices. Change happens slowly, yet it happens. We form alliances and lobby for change. Our early discussions resulted in the International Labour Organization's ratification of Convention #169 on the Rights of Indigenous and Tribal Peoples. More recently, and more consistently, we have met with regard to the *Draft Declaration on the Rights of Indigenous Peoples*. Your family tends to be outside the discussion because most of it takes place not through regular channels but in hotel lobbies and hallways, over coffee or tea, or any place not controlled by the dominant ideology.

We are not involved in a conspiracy to exclude you from the conversation, *Kiciwamanawak*. We want to talk to you, but you will not listen. So we talk to each other. These discussions result in solidarity, an expression of "All My Relations." Through these discussions, Aboriginal peoples are re-learning relatedness. While your family insists on domination and superiority, you deny yourself the experience of belonging. You remain outside the discussion, outside understanding.

CHAPTER SIX

Political Divisions

You and I are in this moment together, *Kiciwamanawak*. We cannot change the past and all the choices made in those moments that led directly to this moment. We live now in a world of artificial structures that make up your society. My family has been pulled into these structures, sometimes by force, so that now many of us accept the structures as real and natural and necessary. It is impossible to think outside the box when we limit our minds to what is inside the box. We cannot think beyond artificial structures if we believe the structures are real or necessary. We can never imagine freedom from artificial prisons.

Some of my relatives now imagine our families joined under a single structure. They imagine a third order of government. They imagine inclusion as distinct peoples of Canada under a single constitution. Before we imagine this, we should look more closely at your political systems. Your system appears to be divided between socialism and capitalism.

The left sprang into prominence with a political philosopher named Karl Marx, who imagined that labourers could and would achieve freedom. He wrote a book called *Das Kapital*, which few people have read but many have died for. Marx tried to explain what was happening in terms of pure economics, and he based his predictions on that. He predicted that labourers would evolve toward communism, a state of being that he was able to imagine by looking at the work of Rousseau, who had studied First Nations traditional ways of being. Marx's collaborator, Friedrich Engels, said that there was a step between capitalism and communism called socialism. Under socialism, labourers would take positions within government and rule on behalf of the labourers rather than the capitalists. The labourers would then prepare the way for communism. Of course, the labourers never achieved communism; they got as far as socialism, then devolved into tyranny. The capitalists continue much as before, except that politics is now split between the left and the right.

The political spectrum is only an idea, a means of imagining what is going on. For most people, it often does not matter which faction — left or right — holds power. The labourer eats the same dust for relatively the same pay, under the same conditions. For the labourer, it seldom matters who has authority over him. It does not matter if the person holding the whip is a socialist or a capitalist; the whip feels the same.

The socialists maintain the same structures created by the capitalists, and they created even more elaborate structures of their own. The left and the right support the same structure: two pillars hold up the weight of tyranny. Tyranny arises among people who rely on structure for their authority. Whenever a person asserts these powers, they point to the text of the structures as authority for their actions.

People who self-identify as leftists occasionally suggest that their ideology and First Peoples' tradition are compatible. They point to their egalitarian hopes to support the suggestion. From a First Nations perspective, however, the left-right political continuum has nothing to do with us. They are the two pillars of your political structure, and only exist in the minds of your own family. Your family tends to think in straight lines. Only linear thought could conceive a straight-line continuum.

If we look at these two ideologies from a First Nations perspective, we would have to change the straight-line continuum into a circle. The circle is representative of First Nations' traditional thought, which is inclusive and holistic. If we place the liberal balance point between left and right at the north of the circle, with the left occupying the northwest quarter and the right occupying the northeast quarter, the First Nations' traditional view would be toward the south. If we follow the leftist view away from the liberal north point, through socialism to communism, we will eventually arrive in the west but headed toward the First Nations' position. Likewise, if we follow the right view away from the centre through *laissez faire* capitalism, we will arrive in the east but headed toward the First Nations' position.

We must remember that this circle is only a mind game. It has no basis in reality, and we should not give it any more reality than it has. The imagined circle is only a way of understanding our differences. Use it if it helps you to understand. If it does not help you, leave it alone.

My family's social organisation does not depend on opposing, adversarial positions. Our social organization begins with a healthy individual, strong in mind, body, and spirit, living in balance with her environment. The individual has choices and accepts the consequences of them. All authority, along with all responsibility, is vested in the individual. The healthy, balanced individual participates freely in family, in community, and the nation; she never surrenders authority or avoids responsibility.

The family, the community, and the nation are all comprised of like individuals joined in a common understanding. Authority is the power of choice; responsibility is the acceptance of the consequences of choice. Together, choice and consequence are for the individual to keep and take care of. If the individual allows another to make choices for him, gives away his authority, he can attempt to avoid responsibility for his choices. Likewise, if we make choices for others, we are responsible for the consequences.

We do not do any favours by making choices for others. If we do it too often, they become dependent on us and never learn to make choices on their own. We must allow each other to make mistakes, so that each of us can learn. We must learn tolerance.

Our social organization does not require any left-right continuum, or dichotomy, or bi-cameral analysis. Each individual is a political entity, a fully emancipated participant. The power of choice is ours alone. How we interact with each other in families, in communities, and in nations is dependent on respect for individual choice and the acceptance of the consequences of our choices. When we interact with others, we must allow them to experience the consequences of their choices. That is the only way they will ever learn to make good choices.

Kiciwamanawak, my experience in your social structure leads me to believe that you do not think about your choice when you give it away to artificial entities such as the church, the state, or the corporation. You seem to find it natural to take away the choice of others and impose codes of order on them. But if you give away your choice, how are you ever going to experience the consequences of that choice? How are you going to learn to be responsible? I do not want to tell you what to do. I do not want to tell you how to live. I do not want that responsibility. I only want to tell you that, if you make good choices, there will be good consequences.

If you keep your authority and take responsibility, there is no one to blame for the negative consequences. At the same time, all the good things in your life are the result of your choices. No one can take those things away from you. You have no human to blame and no human other than yourself to thank for the position you find yourself in this moment.

CHAPTER SEVEN

Resources

THIS IS A GOOD MOMENT. Our Mother the Earth still generously supplies us with all our physical needs. We have air to breathe and water to drink; we are capable of love and kindness and pity. We should be happy. Yet, there is great sorrow in our shared territory, among your family and among mine. Our relatives, *Kiciwamanawak*, do not believe they have any choices. They feel trapped and controlled. For many of them, it has been generations since they had the power of choice. Dependent on churches, governments, and corporations, they have not learned responsibility.

We cannot take down these structures right away; we cannot treat our dependent relatives that badly. The people who receive their privilege and status from the structures will not allow us to tear them down, in any case. It seems, *Kiciwamanawak*, that you and I are stuck with the artificial structures for a little longer.

Many of my family have become dependent on the Department of Indian Affairs, and even though most people now accept that the *Indian Act* is racist and demeaning, we are dependent on it for survival. It represents food and shelter to many of my relatives, and we cannot allow the government to dismantle it. It seems that just enough money flows to my relatives out of the Department of Indian Affairs to keep them dependent, but never enough to allow them to become independent. Why is it that, in such a wealthy territory, people do not have enough and must remain dependent on the government? This dependence began harshly in 1885 when my relatives were confined to their reserves, and a pass system was imposed, presumably to prevent us from joining our relatives the Métis in resistance. Prior to the pass system, we could come and go from our reserves as we chose.

From 1885 until the 1940s, my family had to ask the Indian Agent for a pass to leave the reserve for any reason, even to go hunting or to visit relatives on another reserve. The system was not removed from the *Indian Act* until 1951. We became dependent upon the agent for food, shelter, and clothing.

Our dependence is more than psychological. We have become dependent on you for our very survival. We are still confined by the denial of access to the earth's generosity. We watch from our reserves or inner-city ghettos while the wealth of the territory flows past us. Then we stand in line and wait for our own inadequate share.

It seems that the minor programs we are given to run are set up to fail. It seems that, whenever we try to become independent, we are confronted by laws that limit our incentive.

The exploitation of the earth's wealth becomes more aggressive every year. The corporations seem to be in a feeding frenzy, tearing at the earth's carcass. Mechanical wolves rip her granular flesh to expose uranium in the north; others grind through her body, mulching potash in the south. Oil and gas are sucked from the ground for profit by oil companies. Giant machines tear the coal from her body while prospectors searching for diamonds swarm the territory. The tree line has been pushed north over a hundred miles since your family arrived, *Kiciwamanawak*. The forest falls to mechanical harvesters at an unprecedented rate. Huge areas of deforestation open in the forest every year without regard for the plant nations or the animal nations that live among them. *Kiciwamanawak*, those are our relatives, too. Without the nations of the plant and the animal, neither your family nor mine can survive. We are tied to them as surely as your family is tied to mine.

While our Mother is being raped and robbed before our eyes, we are told that there are shortages of medicine, food, and housing. When we try to obtain the resources necessary for our survival as dignified human beings, we are denied access by laws that reserve the exploitation of the earth's wealth for the wealthy. Why is it, *Kiciwamanawak*, that only those who control huge wealth can access our Mother, and the rest of us must depend on them for table scraps and handouts?

The plight of my family has been known by successive governments since treaty. The Treaty Commissioner promised that we would continue to have what we had and would receive the Queen's bounty and benevolence as well. We have not been allowed to live as we did before. We cannot access a decent livelihood from the earth's plenty. The Queen's bounty and benevolence is just enough to maintain us in perpetual poverty.

Our poverty has been studied in detail by experts who have suggested, among other idiotic notions, that we mortgage our reserves. Our reserves are already too small for survival. The poverty of my family, and the obvious solutions to it, have been known by people in your government for so long that I can only conclude that our poverty has been maintained deliberately.

This is a hard accusation I am making against your family, *Kiciwamanawak*. I am blaming you for our poverty. As a human I should not be able to blame others; I should make choices and accept the consequences. But insofar as your laws limit my choices, insofar as you assume authority over me, insofar as I cannot access the wealth of my Mother the Earth, then you are responsible for my poverty. Because you have known about my poverty for so long and have done nothing about it, you must intend that I live in poverty.

This condition will likely continue. I no longer hope for change in my lifetime. But, if we start now, in this pivotal moment, maybe the future of our children and their children and grandchildren will be better. The cycles of denial and dependence — the denial of choice and the subsequent dependence of my family — have to end. But before that can happen, we have to become healthy and balanced enough to exercise our choices wisely. We cannot learn to make wise choices while others make choices for us. The dilemma is circular. There are no easy, straight-line answers, no formula that will solve it. We have to put our minds and our hearts together and fight the differences between your family and mine. There are no quick fixes. We have to learn to live together as humans, as relatives.

At the negotiation of our treaty, it was clear to both sides that my family was to remain free to access a livelihood from the territory we agreed to share with you. Morris repeatedly made statements of assurance and understanding:

What I have offered does not take away your living, you will have it then as you have now, and what I offer now is put on top of it. This I can tell you, the Queen's Government will always take a deep interest in your living.[31]

And:

We have not come here to deceive you, we have not come here to rob you, we have not come here to take away anything that belongs to you.[32]

Fort Carlton, Saskatchewan, one of the sites of the 1876 negotiation and signing of Treaty No. 6. (Saskatchewan Archives Board, S-B10213.)

And again:

> I again explained that we would not interfere with the Indian's daily life except to assist them in farming.[33]

When it appeared that the Treaty Commissioner did not understand what my family was asking for, our spokesperson the Badger at Fort Carlton clarified:

> I do not want you to feed me every day; you must understand that from what I have said. When we commence to settle down on the ground to make our own living, it is then we want your help. . . .[34]

If we were to be free to live after the treaty as we had lived before it, then we would have access to the resources of our territory. It is no longer possible to make a livelihood from trapping and fishing, though many continue to try. If we are to live as before, independently, not relying on your family for subsistence, then we need access to the resources of our territory. It is a wealthy territory, *Kiciwamanawak*; it has fed, clothed, and housed my family since we were put here. It is only by your regulation of resources that we are denied the self-sufficiency that we were assured at treaty.

Many of the holders of privileged positions in the artificial entities of the state and the corporation have forgotten their connection to the earth. The lumberjack works every day in the forest with a chainsaw. The smell of sawdust and evergreen follows him home. He knows his connection to the earth. It is on his hands and in his nostrils, and very often in his heart. The operator of a mechanical tree harvester is a little further removed. The truck driver who hauls the trees to a mill is further removed still, but not as far as the mill worker who turns the tree into lumber or paper. By the time the paper reaches the academic or the newspaper editor or the stockbroker, all connections to the earth have been forgotten. The miner who drills and blasts the earth has a life-and-death relationship with her. He knows that she can kill him on any given day. But the people who use the copper, the zinc, the gold, or the uranium forget that a man risked his life to rip the ore out of the earth.

Except for sunlight and the odd meteorite, everything comes from our Mother the Earth. All wealth was here at the time of treaty. This territory has provided for all our needs in the past, and it still can in the future. As humans, we are incapable of creating wealth. All we can do is apply our labour to the earth's bounty, modifying it to suit our needs. Banks, casinos, stock markets, and franchises do not generate wealth because they are not real. The people who work inside these artificial structures use the structures themselves to justify their accumulation of wealth.

To understand wealth, we must step back and look at each of our family's laws. As I understand it, my family's law is about the maintenance of harmonious relationships: relationships between me and my family, my community, my nation, my Creator, the four directions, the earth, the plant nations, the animal nations, and your nation.

Your law seems to be about property. Contract law is about the division of property, criminal law is about the protection of property, tort law is about the preservation of property, and tax law is about the redistribution of property.

Under my family's law, wealth is an abundance of good relations — ancestors that prayed for us, children that love us, a community and a nation that accept and respect us. Under your law, wealth seems to be about how much of the earth and her bounty can be accumulated and controlled.

When your laws are applied to my family, they disregard our connections, and often break them. Laws that are designed to regulate hunting, fishing, trapping, and gathering especially break our connection to the earth. The enforcement of the written text of the treaties with regard to "such tracts as may from time to time be taken up for settlement, mining, lumbering or other purposes" directly breaks our connection. The concept of exclusive personal property in tracts of territory held by your family keeps us out of those tracts, whether exclusive property is expressed in homesteads, townships, mineral rights, or forest management leases.

The concept of property is laid over the earth like a sheet of clear plastic: invisible, sterile, and devoid of human connection. Exclusive control and the right to exploit tracts of territory are inconsistent with our agreement to share. Sectioning off almost the entire territory is a direct denial of the promise that we could live as before. How can we live as before, gathering food and medicine, when the territory is criss-crossed with barbed wire, and trespass laws keep my family out?

It is not for me to tell you how to live, *Kiciwamanawak*. You can arrange your family any way you want. You can believe that property is not only a concept, but that it is real, natural, or necessary. You can design complex structures based on property to maintain order within your family. I respect your choice. But I cannot accept that your concepts are superior to mine and should be imposed on my family and me. It would be a dereliction of my duty as a human to allow another to make choices for me, to stand between the Creator and me, or sever my connection to the earth.

I cannot convince myself that your artificial entities are real. I cannot respect them the same as I respect you, *Kiciwamanawak*. I cannot sever my relationship with my Mother, my Creator, my relations, and replace it with devotion to false Gods.

There are many entities that I believe in without logical or physical proof of their existence, but governments, churches, and corporations are not among them. I realize that these entities have achieved near mystical stature in your culture. They hold a special place in your social organization. But my law requires that I relate to entities that have a spirit within them. I recognize the spirits of the West, the North, the East, the South, the Creator, the Earth, and the spirit of this day. I recognize the spirits within plants, within animals, and within you, *Kiciwamanawak*.

When you refer to Crown land, I realize that you do not mean that the Queen herself holds the land. What you are referring to is the ring of gold and jewellery on her head. Crown land is land that is controlled by a piece of jewellery locked away in the Tower of London. This piece of jewellery has mystical powers. The woman who wears it does not use the land it controls; most of it she has never seen. This magical piece of jewellery is used by your family to award themselves and do favours for their friends.

The people who worship the jewellery and are blessed by it also worship pieces of paper called charters and incorporation documents. They use these magical devices to keep me off my Mother the Earth. Only if I have the magic of an incorporation document will the people who are blessed by the power of the jewellery allow me to harvest the bounty of the earth. If I am an incorporated mining company or logging company, then I am allowed to harvest from that portion of the earth controlled by the magic jewellery, Crown land.

Remember, *Kiciwamanawak*, that at the time of treaty, your family came to us and asked to share this territory. We adopted you according to our law and agreed that your family could occupy this territory. But your right to occupy the territory did not give you right to impose your law, your customs, and your religion. What made you assume that your law was superior to ours? What makes you believe that you are superior to nature? Because you can destroy it?

Kiciwamanawak, we are told that there are four colours of humans: black, red, yellow, and white. These match the colours of the four directions, and each colour was given a responsibility by the Creator. My family was given the responsibility to look after the earth. Your family was given the responsibility to look after fire. The black people were given the responsibility to look after water. The yellow people were given the responsibility to look after the air.

My family cannot protect the earth while your fire rages out of control. Your industrial fires have touched every part of the earth and even blasted rockets into space. Your fires have scorched holes in the ozone layer, and the planet is heating up because of your fires. We must come together and find balance. We must rid ourselves of the differences between us before your fire scorches all of Mother Earth.

It seems to me, *Kiciwamanawak*, as I watch your family, that you are like fire. You consume everything. Your family consumes far more than any other family on the planet. You seem driven to consume, to devour. You consume things you do not need, and sometimes even things you do not want. Like a wild fire out of control, you do not seem to look ahead. The hotter you rage, the more you consume.

Your industrial fires have brought many good things: steel, glass, electric light. But the earth provides the fuel for your fires and the ore for your smelters. If your consumption rages out of control much longer, you will scorch the entire earth to the destruction of your family and mine. I have a duty to the next seven generations that I keep the earth for them. I cannot fulfill my duty if I allow you to continue to burn and consume without at least warning you what you are doing.

Kiciwamanawak, we need to find balance. Some of my family have been hypnotized by your flames and have become like you; they have become consumers. Some of your family can see the earth and try to be like my family. They are humans with the gift of choice. Some of my family have chosen to be like yours and some of your family have chosen to be like mine. Neither way is the only way or the correct way for everyone.

Passing more laws to protect the Earth will not work. My family is responsible for the earth. If we depend on your laws and your enforcement, then we have abdicated our sacred duty. This is a duty that each of us carries individually. We must each choose to fulfil it because we each will bear the consequences.

You alone, *Kiciwamanawak*, must choose: consider the earth, consider my family and the other families on the planet, or continue to behave as though there were no tomorrow. If you choose to ignore the earth, there will be no tomorrow.

It seems at times that everyone is in a feeding frenzy, like a pack of dogs ripping at a carcass, blood in their nostrils, minds raging, fighting each other for another mouthful, for another television, another computer, another car. Proclaiming another law will not stop the frenzy. People will always find a way to feed the fire of consumption. But it is individual people who make up the flames. It is individual people who must rediscover their sanity.

This territory is still healthy. It can still provide all we need. But at the present rate of consumption, greed, and waste, I doubt that it can last more than a few generations. We have only to balance our needs with what we take from the earth and she will provide as far into the future as she has into the past.

Our families came together at treaty. We agreed to share this territory. We agreed that your family would bring technology and share it with us as we agreed to share the earth with you. We did not give you control over the entire territory, nor did we abdicate our responsibility for the earth. Under our law, we did not have the right to pass off our duty to your family, to surrender our choice, our authority.

The consequences we face today come from choices made by men. Men have chosen to deforest large areas of this territory. Men have chosen to mine and lay waste the northern portion of this territory. Like many of your family, I have worked as a logger and a miner. I operated a mechanical harvester. I dumped truckload after truckload of radioactive waste upon the earth. The American pulp and paper company never smelled chainsaw exhaust or saw the clear cuts. The uranium mining company never felt the vibration of a drill boring through the heart of our Mother. They could not. They are not real. They are pretensions given legal authority. It was men who decimated this territory, men who believed the companies and corporations were real and would take responsibility for our actions, men who accepted wages and chose to ignore what they were doing. We are responsible, the consequences are ours. Our children and grandchildren will share the consequences.

Under your *Constitution*, resources are the responsibility of the provinces. In this territory, resources were transferred to the province through the *Natural Resource Transfer Agreement, 1930*. This transfer of jurisdiction from the federal government, which is responsible for "Indians and lands reserved for Indians" under section 91(24) of the *Constitution Act, 1867*, to the province, which has no relationship with nor responsibility for First Nations, has been a major source of contention for my family. At treaty we agreed to share; we adopted a new family into the territory. How did the federal government manage to give away more than it possessed?

Since 1930 — and, more rapidly and directly, since 1980 — the Province of Saskatchewan has allowed the exploitation of resources at unsustainable levels. Forestry giants have been allowed to harvest at levels that exceed the capacity of the forest to regenerate itself. Industrial logging has devastated animal populations. The silt that flows into creeks and rivers from mechanized harvesters and the destruction of the forest bed kills the fish. My preferred way of making a living has been destroyed.

If your family is going to assert an absolute right to manage the resources of this territory, then I suggest you do it right. If you are going to take my responsibility to the earth away from me, then you have an obligation to ensure that the earth is well cared for. If you cannot take care of our Mother better than you have, then return jurisdiction over resources to my family.

CHAPTER EIGHT

Taxation

———

MY FAMILY IS OFTEN BLAMED for the tyranny your family experiences at taxation time. "If the Indians didn't get everything for free," they say, "we wouldn't have to pay so much tax." My family did not invent taxation. Taxation is an element of the tyranny of your social structures and your stratified society. Taxation is one of the most complex areas of your legal system. Very few lawyers practice in this area because it requires specialized and continuous training. The rules continuously change and evolve toward greater complexity.

If I were to design a system of taxation, I would return to the basics of your culture and remember that taxation should be about the redistribution of material wealth. From my culture, I would remember that all wealth comes from the earth. Our Mother's bounty is there for all. Taxation at the point of extraction would meet both cultural requirements. It would allow for redistribution of wealth to those not extracting while recognizing the ultimate source of it. It would serve the dual purpose of ensuring that the extractors complied with environmental standards. The bounty of the earth could be distributed without serious disruption to the present social order. It is simple to change tax laws. They change every year as it is.

The earth's bounty is for everyone. Each person should be entitled to equal access and an equal share. People who extract from the earth should share their excess if they extract more than they need. Taxation at the point of extraction can accomplish this sharing of the surplus.

The allegation that my family has an unfair advantage because some of us do not pay tax on some transactions is based on the assumption that the taxation of consumption is natural and necessary. From my family's perspective, it seems absurd that those people who benefit the most from the extraction of the earth's wealth pay minimal tax to encourage them to extract more, while taxation, which is forced sharing, is imposed on consumers.

I suspect that the people who accuse my family of having an unfair advantage are themselves feeling oppressed because they are not receiving what they perceive to be their fair share and, adding insult to injury, they have to pay tax on their share. When a person does not have enough and is forced to share, the burden of sharing through taxation becomes doubly onerous. But many of the people who are oppressed by unfair and illogical taxation policies appear to want my family to be equally oppressed. They forget or ignore that all wealth comes from the earth and that at treaty my family agreed to share the bounty of the earth with your family. We paid our share of taxation for all time when we undertook to share this territory with your family. We were, in effect, taxed again when we were denied access to our share of the earth's bounty. Now some people in your family demand that we pay tax and give back a share of the inadequate amounts transferred to us.

Your family made a treaty with the Anishinabae family before you made a treaty with mine. In the treaty with the Anishinabae, made in 1850, your family promised to pay rent annually for the land leased to your family:

The said William Benjamin Robinson on behalf of Her Majesty, who desires to deal liberally and justly with all of her subjects, further promises and agrees that in case the territory hereby ceded by the parties of the second part shall at any future period produce an amount which will enable the Government of this Province without incurring loss to increase the annuity hereby secured to them, then, and in that case, the same shall be augmented from time to time . . . (With provisos)[35]

In 1867 your family passed the *British North America Act*, which created the nation of Canada. This *Act* set out the respective powers of the new nation and the provinces. One of the powers of the new federal entity was to relate with "Indians and lands reserved for Indians."[36] The governments of Quebec and Ontario argued that, because Canada was responsible for Indians and lands reserved for Indians, the rent owed the Anishinabae under treaty should be paid out of revenue assigned to Canada. The representatives of the three governments — Ontario, Quebec, and Canada — argued the case up to Privy Council in England, which, until 1949, was Canada's final court of appeal. The privy councillors decided that the rent did not have to be paid because the treaties were not real treaties:

> Their Lordships have had no difficulty in coming to the conclusion that, under the treaties, the Indians obtained no right to their annuities, whether original or augmented, beyond a promise and agreement, which was nothing more than a personal obligation by its governor, as representing the old province, that the latter should pay the annuities as and when they became due; that the Indians obtained no right which gave them any interest in the territory which they surrendered, other than that of the province; and that no duty was imposed upon the province, whether in the nature of a trust obligation or otherwise, to apply the revenue derived from the surrendered lands in payment of the annuities. They will, accordingly, humbly advise Her Majesty that the judgement of the Supreme Court of Canada ought to be affirmed, and both appeals dismissed.[37]

This legal precedent has led subsequent lawyers, lawmakers, and bureaucrats to the conclusion that their family is not bound by the treaties, and can change them at any time. In a 1964 decision, J. A. Johnson for the Northwest Territories Court of Appeal, stated, in respect to the Anishinabae case:

> While this refers only to the annuities payable under the treaties, it is difficult to see that the other covenants in the treaties, including the one we are here concerned with, can stand on any higher footing. It is

always to be kept in mind that the Indians surrendered their rights in the territory in exchange for these promises. This "promise and agreement," like any other, can, of course, be breached, and there is no law of which I am aware that would prevent Parliament by legislation, properly within s. 91 of the *B.N.A. Act*, from doing so.[38]

No justification has ever been given by any judge in any Canadian court for the assertion that your family can change the treaties, other than that the British Privy Council once said so.[39] Until the passing of section 35 of the *Constitution Act, 1982*, your government could change the treaties whenever it wanted. Since then, your government has been prohibited from unilaterally altering them, but the changes instituted prior to 1982 have been held to continue to apply. In this context, it seems absurd to argue that my family should pay tax when your family is more than a century behind in rent.

Kiciwamanawak, you can arrange your family any way you want. You can use taxation as a means of redistributing wealth among your family members. You can use the revenue from taxation to pay for elaborate, artificial structures. You can insist that the poorest people in your family contribute to the maintenance of those structures. But you have no right to impose your structures and your methods of financing those structures on my family. You cannot at once maintain us in perpetual poverty and demand that we return a portion of the little we have to support your structures.

CHAPTER NINE

Assimilation

KICIWAMANAWAK, WE HAVE TO TALK about your family's policy of assimilation. This constant effort to make us change into you, to become like you, to adopt your structures and forget what we know to be true, has caused extreme hurt to my family. The policy of assimilation has not worked, does not work, and will not work. You have been trying for hundreds of years. Give it up. When we lose our culture, our traditions, our knowledge and understanding, we do not become you. Your family has learned your culture since the beginning of time. Your culture goes back to Genesis and the Garden of Eden. You have had a long time to learn it. Now your culture is so much a part of who you are that many of your family do not even see it. They decry that they have no culture and seek out other families' cultures. This denial seems to arise out of your family's insistence on supremacy. You deny that you are a product of your culture, or any culture, to enhance the appearance of purity. You prefer to describe your way of doing things as scientific or logical rather than merely cultural. To many of your family, it seems that culture is what lesser peoples have.

You and I have different ways of being on the earth. Your perspective springs, in part, from Genesis 1:28, where God blessed Adam and Eve and told them to "be fruitful and multiply, and fill the earth and subdue it; and have dominion over the fish of the sea and over the birds of the air and over every living thing that moves upon the earth." The word "dominion" may not be an accurate translation from the Hebrew. It might be better translated as "caretaker" or "steward," which would be closer to my understanding of our relationship with the earth. I am a grandchild of the earth. I am not her master.

Your family has had thousands of years to develop your perspective as masters of the earth. I recognize that it might be difficult for you to abandon your high seat and view the world from ground level. I do not expect you to. I only ask that you realize that other people see the world from different positions and have different perspectives that are equally valid. You have no monopoly on vision.

Your family's attempt to force the rest of the world to see things your way has had devastating results. The affects of colonization have been studied and debated at least since Albert Memmi's insightful *The Colonizer and the Colonized* was first published in 1957.[40] Despite nearly half a century of discussion, however, little has changed. The colonial perspective continues to dominate. The truly sad aspect of this is that the perspective is so limited. It is primarily an economic vision, a masculine vision, and it is very short-sighted. It cannot see beyond the next stock market crash. It does not even pretend to see beyond our children to our grandchildren, and certainly cannot see seven generations ahead. Today, we are expected to accept the dominant perspective simply because it is dominant.

There does not seem to be room for any other view. Your markets rule, your bicameral government is proposed as the ultimate style, while your democracy — the freedom to participate in markets, food markets, house markets, clothing markets, labour markets — is forced upon the rest of the world. Your perspective seems blind to those without food, houses, clothing, or a job.

Kiciwamanawak, you have two eyes so that you can perceive depth. Because your eyes are slightly apart, you can better judge distance. Imagine if you had many eyes, all focused on the same object from different directions, how clear and complete your vision might be.

From your single view, you perceive yourselves as the greatest race on earth. While people in your government promote this territory as the best place in the world to live, they forget to mention child prostitution, solvent abuse, youth gangs, housing shortages, devastated ecological zones, diminishing natural resources, the collapsing rural community, poisoned water, people who are dependent upon a shaky health care system for their survival, and a government that is financially dependent on casinos.

Kiciwamanawak, why do you insist that I become like you? Your vision is uniquely yours, but it is no more valid than anyone else's. If individualization, competition, and adversarialism work for you, that's fine. But others prefer community, co-operation, and healing.

J. M. Blaut has convincingly shown in *The Colonizer's Model of the World*[41] that your family did not make the advancements in agriculture and technology that you claim. Those advancements were made by other families and appropriated by yours. Sákéj Henderson, a human rights lawyer who teaches in the Native Law Centre at the University of Saskatchewan, and Marie Battiste, a professor in the Indian and Northern Education Program at the same university, have detailed the theft of Indigenous knowledge by your family. I will not repeat what these people have said. I only suggest that you read their words with an open mind.[42] Take an honest look at your history and you will see that the advancements that you claim are not yours. Take an honest look at your family today before you insist that the rest of the world adopt your family structure. Before you deliberately destroy my family's way of being upon the earth, you should come to understand our way.

Your scientists have only begun to study ecology, and very few have opened their hearts to it. Your scientists have spent even less time studying complexity, finding order within chaos. My family has studied ecology and complexity for thousands of years, with our minds, our hearts, and our bodies. Our understanding has been detailed in our stories, and in our ceremonies. We have had the advantage of generations of study to begin our own personal studies as we seek to develop our own understanding of our place within the ecological order of our total environment.

Once set upon this path of understanding, once a person experiences the freedom of choice and consequence, once a person experiences balance between men and women, between themselves and their family, their community, their nation, between past, present, and future, between themselves and the different directions, then your structures appear simplistic and tyrannical — simplistic because you depend solely on logic for their justification, rather than including experience and emotion as ways of knowing. You will never understand water until you experience thirst. You will never understand food until you experience hunger. You will never understand "All My Relations" until you experience yourself. Your dependence on logic as justification for your tyrannical structures is simplistic, masculine, and limited when compared with other ways of knowing. Your singular view of the world is not superior merely because it is exclusive. Logic is not purer because it ignores other ways of knowing. Your lines of authority, your linear explanations, your social structures and boxes and assembly lines are all based on mechanical logic, exclusive of the psychological, emotional, and spiritual experiences of both men and women.

Your family's insistence that everyone adopt bicameral, multi-party, adversarial government, that everyone participate in your markets, that everyone be like you, agree with you, destroys all other ways of knowing, of being. The result will be uniculture, and from our study of ecology we know that a single, isolated species is the most vulnerable. Continued assimilation will result in the destruction of us all.

I accept your way of being, *Kiciwamanawak*. I accept that your way is the best way for you to be in this moment. I do not wish to change you or your social structures. I need you to be different from me. The more ways of seeing, the more ways of being, the surer the future for our children and grandchildren, and their grandchildren. You have something to contribute to future generations that should be more than an example of how not to be. I hope seven generations in the future that they do not look back at us, *Kiciwamanawak*, and say, "Let's not make the same mistakes they made."

CHAPTER TEN

Leadership

It seems urgent to me, *Kiciwamanawak*, that we stop perpetuating imbalance and begin to facilitate the restoration of balance. My family has experienced generations of interference, denial of access, imposed authority, and relinquishment of responsibility. It will take generations until we are healthy, happy, and once again understand our place in the great mystery. We need your restraint and your co-operation.

Kiciwamanawak, we need you to stop imposing your way of being and allow us our share of the bounty of our Mother the Earth.

We do not have an equivalent phrase for "excuse me" in our language. We do not know how to politely ask you to step out of the way. We did not develop the phrase because we have never needed it. We have a history of non-interference, of not standing in each other's way. We know how to walk around each other. In our tradition, the rudest behaviour is to step over another person. Anyone who would do that was likely to step over people in other ways also.

In my family's tradition, no one has rights above another. We are all equal seekers of understanding, seekers of good health and happiness, balanced in this moment in our total environment. From what I have been told, we did not have a full-time chief. We occasionally had an *Okamaw*, which is not a boss or a sovereign, but rather a leader. When we were faced with war, we would ask our best warrior to be *Okamaw*, to lead the warriors. We were not at war often. That is a lie your family tells about us. We did have occasion to fight when another group of people moved into the territory that we relied on for our survival. Our wars did not become brutal and deadly until your family arrived. Prior to contact with your family, our wars were more about proving bravery than about killing each other.

When our dispute with another group was finished, when we pushed them out of the territory, or they pushed us out, we would allow our *Okamaw* to become one of the people again. Likewise, in a time of poor hunting, we would ask our best hunter, someone the spirits smiled upon, to be *Okamaw* for the hunt, to lead the hunters. Again, when the hunt was over, the greatest reward we gave the *Okamaw* was to let him become one of the people again.

We recognized that authority and responsibility are onerous and should not be imposed on a person for too long. It is a heavy burden to carry the authority and responsibilities of others, and if we give away our personal authority and responsibilities, we avoid our duty as humans. We had many *Okamawak* (the plural) in our societies. Among the young, the oldest in the group took responsibility for the safety of the younger. I understand that among the women there were leaders, but because I am a man I do not know enough to comment. Among the variety of *Okamawak*, none had anything approaching absolute authority. These were people who were respected for their abilities rather than their lineage or accumulated wealth.

My family's way of social organization was first to identify an objective, then to create the minimal social structure necessary to accomplish it. Everyone knew the work to be done, and everyone participated. Leaders were not necessary in most circumstances. Each person was respected for his or her abilities and allowed to contribute to the whole. The minimal structure necessary was often for one or more persons to lead the way, to take responsibility based on their unique gift or ability. We did not select leaders *ad hoc*. We had entire lifetimes to evaluate gifts and abilities. Only a person who walked in the world in a good way, who had a sincere prayer and received the blessing of their ancestors, would be asked to be *Okamaw*.

For objectives that affected everyone, the entire community participated in the selection of *Okamaw*. The selection process required the evaluation of the potential *Okamaw* and his entire life. The oldest, most experienced and respected men and women were relied upon for their judgement in the selection. But ultimately, the entire community assented to the *Okamaw*.

An *Okamaw* did not have privilege, was not bowed down to, and had no more authority over anyone than that person gave to him. An *Okamaw* was a leader, not a commander. The people followed the *Okamaw* of their choice. Their choice was determined by the amount of respect an *Okamaw* was able to garner, how well he protected and provided. An *Okamaw* was evaluated not only on how well he led, but also on how he lived, how he walked in the world every day, how he treated his family, his children, his wife or wives, and how well he listened.

Before a major decision was made, an *Okamaw* listened to what everyone had to say. Some people's opinions were held in higher regard than others. The elders, the thinkers, and people who were gifted could be sure that they were consulted, and their opinions given due consideration. But ultimately, everyone participated; everyone contributed to any major decision. After an *Okamaw* listened to everyone, the choice was his. Everyone having contributed to the decision accepted the decision, usually even if his or her personal opinion was not the choice of the *Okamaw*. Consensus does not mean that everyone agrees, only that everyone participates and accepts the final decision.

If a person strongly opposed the choice of the *Okamaw*, which was rare, that person was free to leave, sometimes alone, sometimes with a group of like-minded people. Everyone was free to leave at any time. The only power an *Okamaw* had was what his respect earned him. The people followed an *Okamaw* out of choice, not out of coërcion.

Most of the time an *Okamaw* could not be differentiated from anyone else. He was allowed to be one of the people and was not needed for day-to-day decisions. Your family may have got the wrong impression when you arrived here and we asked our *Okamawak* to speak for us. The first person your family would have spoken to would have been an *Okamaw*. Whenever you came back, the same *Okamaw* came forward to speak with you. What you would not have seen was that, when you left, the *Okamaw* became just another person. Your family, being accustomed to chiefs and kings and queens and privilege, likely assumed the same was true of us.

When your ancestors came to us, it was always our men who came to meet you, the protectors and providers. Again, based on your own society, you assumed that we treated our women as inferior, that they were not a part of decision-making. *Kiciwamanawak*, we knew for generations that

Cree and Assiniboine council, North-West Territories, circa 1878-79. This is what government looked like prior to colonial rule: people sitting together, close to the earth, not faced off against each other. I suspect this photo shows only a portion of the circle. (Glenbow Archives, na-5501-1.)

you were coming. We were told ahead of time to get ready. The Anishina-bae people began moving west long before your family reached the shores of Turtle Island because they knew you were coming.

When your family arrived in this territory, some of the Anishinabae people were living here. My family, the Nihiyaw, were told long before your arrival that you were on your way. We knew what we were going to say to you when you got here. Our hope was that we could live like two families, two nations, two peoples in the same territory.

Even though we knew you were coming and had generations to prepare, we did not expect that you would relegate our proud, independent family to the lowest ranks of your stratified society.

My ancestors, who prayed for me seven generations ago, never expected that your family would assume control over where I could or could not live, when and how much I hunted, how I prayed, and even who I am related to.[43] No one expected that you would claim all medicines as your own and pass laws against any that were not to your liking. My ancestors who prayed for me never expected that I would have to ask your family's permission to get my food, to cut a tree for firewood, to build a home, to get married, to educate my children, to travel, or to live in the same community as my relatives.

Kiciwamanawak, your way of being is not the only way. I accept that it is the dominant way, but I do not accept that it is the best way. If I say negative things about your family, it is not meant to make you feel bad. Rather, it is to show you that your family is not superior. When I travel through your cities I am not impressed by your building; I am saddened by the destruction. You seem to have forgotten that our Mother lies beneath the concrete and the asphalt. I see hungry, homeless people begging in your streets. Even the people who have homes and jobs seem to live a life of misery, constantly striving to earn enough to survive. I see little happiness or contentment. Many of your family use alcohol or drugs just to get through the day. Sometimes, one of your family goes on a killing spree. Have you ever wondered why there are so many serial killers in industrial societies?

I only want to point out to you, *Kiciwamanawak*, that your family is human, that your social structures are designed by humans. Humans make mistakes. It is okay to be human. We all are. We get into trouble when we forget to be humans and try to be perfect, or when we believe that we are perfect, or that there are other people who are perfect. There are no superior humans. We are all equally human with the human ability to make mistakes. No one was born superior to you, *Kiciwamanawak*. We are all just people. We are all just humans. Maybe if you quit believing in superior humans above you, you might stop trying to be superior over me.

When my ancestors adopted your ancestors as our relatives, they adopted people — not structures, not government, not tyranny. They adopted your Queen as a relative, not a piece of jewellery. They did not adopt your symbols or your corporations or your churches. They adopted people. They adopted you, *Kiciwamanawak*.

I understand that you teach children that your society is based, in part, on the writings of a Greek philosopher named Plato, who proposed a republic ruled by philosopher kings. His republic was stratified into gold, silver, and bronze or iron people. The economics of your system mandate that there will always be less fortunate members. In a competitive system, there must always be losers, or else there can be no winners.

Kiciwamanawak, you have lived a long time with tyranny, with the belief that some people are worth more than others. I understand why you must always find someone beneath you; it is so that you do not feel that you are on the bottom. I suspect that you have treated my family poorly because you needed us to fill the space at the bottom of your hierarchy so that you would not fill it yourself.

Something amazing happens when healthy people come together in a good way, something that is more than the sum of the happiness that each brought. It affects everyone and heightens each person's sense of belonging. When people come together in an unstructured, non-hierarchical gathering for a common purpose they come away with a sense of belonging. They share their happiness and good thoughts with each other.

A woman from your family named Mother Teresa, who lived and worked with some of the poorest people on the planet, once said that the greatest sickness of humanity was loneliness. Your structures, based on competition and individualism, do not alleviate loneliness; they exacerbate it. Before your family and mine can live together in this territory we must each know that we belong here and the other equally belongs here. We must come together as humans, not as subjects.

It was once explained to me that men are like dogs or horses in our understanding, but if we prayed hard and sacrificed, we could achieve the understanding a woman has. Women understand the earth. They are both female, capable of generating, of carrying, and bringing forth life. We are all part of the great mystery of life, and women carry that mystery. They know about giving life. Men are only capable of destroying it. We kill our plant and animal relatives as well as each other.

But life needs death. Life and death are balanced in the cycles of the earth and time. Everything dies, is supposed to die, was born to die. Men and women, the takers and givers of life, must be in balance. *Kiciwamanawak*, prior to your family's assumption of domination over my family, we knew the power and importance of women, of life. It is only after decades of the *Indian Act*, of missionaries, of residential schools, of television, that we have begun to emulate your devaluation of women. I suspect that church doctrine played a role in the devaluation. But I really do not understand how my family came to look down on women and so quickly adopt your gender stratification.

At one time in my family, it was accepted that a woman owned the home and everything in it. If a man left or was put out, he took only his personal possessions. Was it the introduction of private property brought by male fur traders that shifted the balance? Did our men, on selling fur to your family, accumulate so much personal wealth that they exceeded the women's wealth? I do not know the answers to these questions. All that I know is that I grew up in an age when women were and are treated as lower-class people. The male/female balance, so necessary for life, has tilted in favour of men, in favour of death. Women's understanding has been ignored, and we need as many ways of knowing as possible if we are going to see into the future and prepare for the next seven generations. We need what women know.

Kiciwamanawak, why don't you put your law to good use? There are over 500 of my sisters missing in Western Canada. Use your law enforcement people to find my sisters instead of locking up people who were drunk on alcohol that was sold to them by your government. My family has suffered greatly over the past century, but my sisters have suffered more than anyone else. Their deaths have been ignored, their disappearances accepted, their murderers given light jail sentences. In this age, when members of your family are clamouring for more severe punishments for virtually every crime, why do the murderers of my sisters receive only minimal sentences?

Women are the backbone of my family. They need to be strong and healthy so that our children are strong and healthy, so that our future is assured. Women are not just child-bearers, baby machines, and housekeepers. They have an understanding that comes with the ability and experience of giving life. They know more than we do, and they know it intuitively. *Kiciwamanawak*, we adopted each other at treaty. My sisters are your relatives also. As relatives, they should be treated with far more respect than they receive. I wonder, *Kiciwamanawak*, did disrespect for the earth begin at the same time as disrespect for women?

If we are to survive into the future, we have to find balance: balance between your family and mine, balance between us and the earth, and balance between men and women. The future is our responsibility. We stand at a pivotal moment in time. What we do now will determine the future, as the past has determined this moment. We can do nothing to change the past. All we can do is give thanks for the prayers that were said for us, and try to learn from it.

We cannot live in the future, for payday or retirement. Neither can we live in the past, whether they were glory days or days of regret. All we have is this moment to make choices. We can choose to save the earth for the next generations, or we can choose to do nothing. We can choose to respect life, respect the earth, respect women, and try to learn about balance. Regardless of what you do, you will make a choice this moment and you alone are responsible for the consequences of it. This is the Creator's law. This is the law under which we entered treaty.

The treaties are the foundation of your family's occupation of this territory. Without the treaties, your family has no valid justification for its use of the territory. It is only by your treaty right that you have the wealth you enjoy, the standard of living you enjoy. Your acknowledgment of the treaties as first documents will begin to put us back in balance. When your family accepts that this country's founding families are yours and mine, then we can begin to search for other truths.

So far, we are so completely out of balance that we will take a long time to rediscover the equilibrium necessary for our continued survival. We can begin, in this moment, by trying to imagine seven generations ahead. We can begin by recognizing that we are responsible, at this moment, for the choice we make at this moment. We can begin by taking back the authority we have given away. Each of us is responsible for the state of the world; we cannot blame others. We are responsible because we have chosen to accept it.

To get to the future, we need a vision, then we must imagine the steps we must take to get to that vision. We cannot ignore our vision because it seems utopian, too grand, unachievable. Neither can we refuse to take the first steps because they are too small, too inconsequential. Our vision and the way we walk toward that vision will determine who we are. If we have a good vision and walk with truth and honesty toward that vision, then our lives will have purpose and meaning.

We will both be part of whatever future we create, *Kiciwamanawak*. I do not expect you to follow my vision any more than I can follow yours. My vision involves living close with the spirit of the earth, unencumbered by material possessions. I do not expect that you can or would want to live like I do. Your vision is different. What we need to resolve is how we can both have our visions and walk toward them without interference from each other. How do we share this territory so that the spirit of Mother Earth survives?

CHAPTER ELEVEN

Sovereignty

YOUR LAW ACKNOWLEDGES INTERNATIONAL LAW, or the law between sovereign states. In this law, your family asserts sovereignty over this territory and over ~~our laws ignore them~~ is designed by your family as an excuse to ignore my family.

About twenty years after Columbus floundered on the shore of Turtle Island, the pope declared that we were human. Before that, we were treated and killed like animals. The papal declaration had a powerful impact. People in your family needed a rationalization for their actions toward us. They had to treat us like humans and justify what became murder and robbery, which would not have been the case had we remained animals.

The wealth from the "New World" had already begun to flow to the old world. A legal rationalization was necessary to continue the flow of wealth. At the time, Europe was an amalgamation of princes and monarchs loosely united by a common faith, as represented by the pope in Rome.

Your family's population had been devastated by a series of plagues. Your agriculture was primarily oats, wheat, and barley. It was not until contact with Turtle Island that your family learned about healthy food production and began importing corn, beans, squash, potatoes, tomatoes, and cabbage. With the importation of healthy new foods, the population began to increase. The wealth flowing from Turtle Island financed the developments that your family takes pride in. Today your home territory is one of the wealthiest in the world. But the wealth did not originate there. The wealth of your family came from the colonization of the American continents.

The pope's declaration that my family was human threatened to stop the flow of wealth. A Spanish Dominican priest, Franciscus de Victoria (or Vitoria), made up a new theory of law shortly after the pope's declaration. His two surviving works, *On the Indians Lately Discovered* and *On the Law of War Made by the Spaniards on the Barbarians*, are recognized by legal scholars as the foundation of International Law.[44]

De Victoria, a professor of theology at the University of Salamanca, developed International Law theory as a justification for the Spanish portion of your family's forced importation of wealth. It was de Victoria who proposed the concept of sovereignty. He first acknowledged that we were human and capable of owning property. Then he created a legal justification to take away that property. His theory of sovereignty was created by looking at your family and your laws. Basically, he said that your family had sovereignty and my family did not. His theory of sovereignty resulted in sovereignty meaning any state that looked and behaved like a state within your family. All other families were denied the rights associated with sovereignty. De Victoria's theory took away some of the power of the pope, but left intact human law and added international law to the law system of your family.[45]

The wealth from the American continents fundamentally changed the old world system. A merchant class developed with new wealth equal to, or nearly equal to, that of the old monarchs. The power of the pope diminished, along with the power of the monarchs, as huge amounts of precious metals and other wealth flowed across the ocean.

Sovereignty doctrine facilitated the flow of wealth by giving unique powers to your family to rule my family in the perceived absence of my family's ability to rule itself. My family did not have a tyrannical, hierarchical order, and were for that reason deemed unable to handle our own affairs. Sovereignty doctrine allowed for exploitation by the sovereign of the new territory and denied my family any right to interfere in it.

Sovereignty doctrine has continued from the time of Victoria, and now forms the basis of modern International Law. It can still be defined as your family, or any family that looks like your family, in relation to a given territory and the forced exclusion or subjugation of others within that territory.[46]

Kiciwamanawak, you no longer need sovereignty doctrine to justify taking what you need from this territory. You have a treaty right to occupy and use this territory. You received that right when my family adopted yours. Sovereignty is an old excuse to deny my family's equality with yours. Your family has sovereignty and mine does not. But all that sovereignty means is that a family's system of self-governing originated in Europe.

Your constitution is based on this belief in sovereign superiority. Between the time of Victoria and now, the English philosopher John Locke proposed a new theory of your family's social order. He first dispelled the notion that kings received their authority to rule from God. He then proposed that your family formed its civil society because, without a sovereign, your family members would kill each other off fighting over property. His theory was that you formed a social contract, and each of your family implicitly or explicitly consented to the sovereign's power. Locke never admitted to writing the new theory in his lifetime, and we only know it was him from a codicil to his will in which he made the admission.[47]

Locke attacked my family in support of his theory. We became the negative example of what happens when there is no sovereign to keep control. He distorted the truth about my family to such an extent that, on reading his theory, his hatred for us becomes clear:

> For by the Fundamental Law of Nature, Men being to be preserved, as much as possible, when all cannot be preserv'd, the safety of the Innocent is to be preferred: And one may destroy a Man who makes war upon him, or has discovered an Enmity to his being, for the same Reason, that he may kill a Wolf or a Lyon; because such men are not under the ties of the Common Law of Reason, have no other rule, but that of Force and Violence, and so may be treated as Beasts of Prey, those dangerous and noxious Creatures, that will be sure to destroy him, whenever he falls into their power.[48]

And again:

> For I aske whether in the wild woods of uncultivated wast of America left to Nature, without any improvement, tillage or husbandry, a thousand acres will yield the needy and wretched inhabitants as many conveniences of life as ten acres of equally fertile land doe in Devonshire where they are well cultivated.[49]

I have never understood Locke's hatred of my family. He never set foot on Turtle Island, and I am certain that my family never did him any wrong. Yet his theory of property as the basis of your family's social contract enforces the right of the sovereign to take or control all wealth from the earth to the exclusion of my family.

John Locke's social contract has become the theory of the modern constitution. Today, constitutional documents have replaced the monarch as the sovereign. But sovereign power, as articulated by de Victoria, continues to be relied on to exclude my family from the earth's wealth.

Kiciwamanawak, you can arrange your family any way you like; that is none of my concern. You can believe that a piece of paper, your constitution, is your equivalent to an *Okamaw*. You can maintain your theory of constitutional sovereignty and run your family's affairs according to that theory. You will not be in breach of the Creator's law. Those are your choices, and you alone bear the consequences of them.

But, *Kiciwamanawak*, my family did not adopt a piece of paper; they adopted you. The paper at treaty was ancillary to ceremony. My ancestors recognized your paper as your ceremony and participated so as not to offend.

I cannot accept that your constitutional documents have any power. They are inanimate. I cannot talk to those papers and tell them of the plight of my family. I can only talk to you, *Kiciwamanawak*, and remind you that you have treaty rights. I recognize that you have elaborate paper ceremonies and that is how your family does things. My family also has ceremonies; we have our own way of doing things. I have no right to say your paper is wrong or that you are foolish to worship it. I must recognize your choice because it is you who will bear the consequences.

CHAPTER TWELVE

Your Constitution

THE LAST TIME YOUR FAMILY CHANGED your paper *Okamaw* was in 1982. The *Constitution Act, 1982* begins with the words, "Whereas Canada is founded upon principles that recognize the supremacy of God and the rule of law." I must congratulate you, *Kiciwamanawak*. This is a good start. This is what I have been talking about: the Creator's law and your law, two families sharing this territory under treaty. The treaties are under the Creator's law. They are forever. We cannot change them because those promises were made to the spirits of the sun, the grass, and the river (water), which are part of the Creator.

To the extent that your *Constitution* recognizes those forces of the Creator, it is consistent with my family's understanding. I cannot say that the Creator's law is superior to your *Constitution*. To my understanding, the Creator's law does not have hierarchies, one law superior to another. It is more like ecology, in which everything is related to everything else. It is about those relationships. In relation to your *Constitution*, the Creator's law is simply about how you and I are related to each other. The statement that begins your *Constitution*, that your family recognizes the supremacy of God, is a good step toward recognizing that both your family and mine are under the law of the Creator.

Your family's constitution as your sovereign, as your *Okamaw*, as your ideological replacement of a human monarch, cannot give any rights to my family. We already have all of the rights and responsibilities of the Creator's law. We are already equal to you. Now we have to figure out how we are going to live together and share this territory, how our families are going to relate to each other. Our relationship, like all relationships, is under the law of the Creator.

Your Supreme Court consistently misunderstands treaties. Justice Cory, in a decision about my family's hunting for food, mistakenly assumed that your *Constitution* was superior to the treaties. He assumed that the agreement between your federal government and the provinces of Manitoba, Saskatchewan, and Alberta — The Natural Resources Transfer Agreement (NRTA) — could modify the treaties. He wrote:

> If this was the intention, and I conclude that it was, then the proper characterization of the relationship between the *NRTA* and the Treaty rights is that the sole source for a claim involving the right to hunt for food is the *NRTA*. The Treaty rights have been subsumed in a document of a higher order. The Treaty may be relied on for the purpose of assisting in the interpretation of the *NRTA*, but it has no other legal significance.[50]

This assumption is an impossibility. The *Constitution* of Canada cannot modify the treaties because the treaties are the source of justification for your right to be here, your right to have a constitution. Your *Constitution* cannot abrogate treaties because your *Constitution* is your treaty right.

Your *Constitution* cannot take away anything my family does not chose to surrender. If we agree to live together under a single set of rules, then we must agree upon those rules. Your *Constitution* can form the basis of that agreement if it is modified substantially to conform with the treaties.

Section 1 of your *Constitution* guarantees rights and freedoms subject to limits prescribed by law. This section has been used by judges in your courts to take away rights and freedoms based on their perception of what might be justified. To bring this section into conformity with the treaties, you will have to rewrite it to guarantee rights and freedoms subject to the limits of the treaties.

Section 2 of your *Constitution* purports to set out fundamental freedoms. It guarantees freedom of conscience and religion, freedom of thought, belief, opinion, and expression, including freedom of the press, freedom of peaceful assembly, and freedom of association. To bring this section into conformity with the treaties will require the addition of many more fundamental freedoms, such as freedom to gather food, freedom to own a home, freedom to raise children, freedom to access the bounty of Mother Earth, and freedom to be human.

A right to clean air and clean water should supersede freedom of the press. I notice that your family places great faith in a free press as something fundamental to your society. The myth that has been fed to the rest of the world is that the press is the protector of democracy, and that any restriction on it inevitably leads to tyranny. But the protection is so narrow as to be almost meaningless. The rule prevents the government from silencing the press, but does nothing to prevent the press from being manipulated by forces within or outside government. Capital interests commonly influence the press in their favour without sanction or even comment. The press is the great protector of the *status quo*, even when the *status quo* is at worst tyranny and, at best, merely the promotion of élite interests.

The press is free to use its influence to support racist, supremacist, sexist, colonial, and nationalistic views. It is free from responsibility. While the press can serve a useful purpose, it can also be destructive. While it can draw attention to important issues, it more commonly follows gossip and stardom. While it can be artistic, it is more commonly pornographic.

Sections 3, 4, and 5 of your *Constitution* set out how you will run your elections and how you will form and select government. As long as this only refers to how your family will select government, then it requires no modification. The treaties do not interfere in how each family will run itself. However, if we are to have a single government for both families, we will have to decide how each family participates in that government.

Section 6 of your *Constitution* sets out mobility rights for your family. This section conforms with the treaties. You have the right to move and obtain a livelihood in any part of our shared territory. It is worth mentioning that my family also has the right to move and obtain a livelihood anywhere in the shared territory.

Section 7 of your *Constitution* declares that everyone has the right to life, liberty, and security of the person, and the right not to be deprived of those rights except in accordance with the principles of fundamental justice. If by "fundamental justice" you are referring to the Creator's law, then this section conforms to the treaties. However, if "fundamental justice" means "according to your family's rules," then it is one-sided and does not conform with the treaties. Who is going to decide what "fundamental justice" means? Whose principles of fundamental justice are we going to rely on, yours or mine?

Section 8 declares that everyone has the right to be secure against unreasonable search or seizure. Section 9 declares that everyone has the right not to be arbitrarily detained or imprisoned. From my perspective, all of my family members in your prisons have been arbitrarily put there. They were put there by a member of your family based on rules created by your family, rules justified only by your family's perceptions and your family's assumption of superiority. To bring these sections of the *Constitution* into conformity with the treaties, they have to be read keeping in mind that the words "reasonable" and "arbitrary" have to be defined with regard to two families' perceptions and not just those of the judges of your family's courts.

The written text of Treaty No. 6 specifies:

And the undersigned Chiefs on their own behalf and on behalf of all other Indians inhabiting the tract within ceded, do hereby solemnly promise and engage to strictly observe this Treaty, and also to conduct and behave themselves as good and loyal subjects of Her Majesty the Queen.

They promise and engage that they will in all respects obey and abide by the law, and they will maintain peace and good order between each other, and also between themselves and other tribes of Indians, and between themselves and others of Her Majesty's subjects, whether Indians or whites, now inhabiting or hereafter to inhabit any part of the said ceded tracts, and that they will not molest the person or property of any inhabitant of such ceded tracts, or the property of Her Majesty the Queen, or interfere with or trouble any person passing or travelling through the said tracts, or any part thereof, and that they will aid and assist the officers of Her Majesty in bringing to justice and punishment any Indian offending against the stipulations of this Treaty, or infringing the laws in force in the country so ceded.

If we are to give meaning to this section, we have to assume that my family retained jurisdiction to maintain peace and good order between ourselves and others. Only in the event that a member of my family molests the person or property of an inhabitant of the territory or the property of the Crown, or interferes with or troubles a person passing or travelling through the territory, does my family have an express obligation to assist the police. The agreement to assist cannot be read to mean submission. The word is "assist," not "submit." In order to assist in justice, we have to be involved jurisdictionally. When we interpret this section, we must keep in mind that the only laws in force in the country so ceded at the time of treaty were our laws.

Fort Pitt, one of the locations of the 1876 negotiation and signing of Treaty No. 6. (Saskatchewan Archives Board, S-B99.)

This section retains my family's jurisdiction to maintain peace and good order not only over ourselves, but also over "others of Her Majesty's subjects, whether Indians or whites, now inhabiting or hereafter to inhabit any part of the said ceded tracts." This portion of the treaty gives my family jurisdiction over your family. The way this section should work in reality is as follows: if a member of your family commits a crime against another member of your family, then your family can invoke your system of justice and punishment. If a member of your family commits a crime against my family, we have jurisdiction to arrest the individual, but we turn the person over to your system for justice and punishment. If a member of my family commits a crime against another member of my family, my family has jurisdiction to find a solution. If a member of my family offends against the treaty, molests the person or property of any inhabitant of such ceded tracts, or the property of Her Majesty the Queen, or interferes with or troubles any person passing or travelling through the said tracts, or any part thereof, then your justice system has jurisdiction, dependent upon our aid, assistance, and participation.

Sections 10, 11, 12, 13, and 14 of your *Constitution* set out the rights of people brought before your courts on criminal charges. These sections reiterate those principles that were developed by judges in your courts. They are restatements of the common law, and, as such, are simply statements of your family's law. To bring these sections into conformity with the treaties, there will have to be a declaration that my family's laws are equally applicable.

Section 15 is an interesting section. It is in two parts. In the first subsection, it purports to declare that all people are equal before and under the law. Then, in the second subsection, it allows your family to make laws to ameliorate inequality where those laws in themselves cause inequality. To bring this section into conformity with the treaties will require an acknowledgment that my family is already equal and has equal laws. We cannot be equal and be under your laws at the same time. As the section now reads, it assumes the superiority of your law over my family, and states that only your law can ameliorate that inequality.

Sections 16 to 23 set out your family's language rights. Your family presently uses two languages, English and French. How you work out between yourselves which language you will use is up to you. English and French are similar and have many words in common. They are not any more different from each other than Cree is from Anishinabae. If we truly desire to have a multi-linguistic *Constitution*, we should include all Aboriginal languages.

Your *Constitution* indicates that language is extremely important to you, *Kiciwamanawak*. Eight out of 52 sections ensure equality between English and French. Language is important to my family, also. Our language contains all the knowledge and understanding that my family has accumulated since creation. It is a language that best describes processes. English and French are noun-based languages that best describe objects. Our common relatives, the Métis, developed a language that combined our language of process with your language of objects to create a language that suited their experience and understanding. They used my family's language for the accuracy of verbs and your family's language for precise nouns. Their language, like my family's language, is threatened and may disappear without intervention and protection.

My family's language has been attacked and threatened with eradication. Residential schools strapped our language right out of our mouths. When I attended grade school, we were strapped if we spoke our language anywhere in the school yard, even on weekends. If we were hurt during play, we had to remember to say "Ouch" instead of "Iyaya." Our parents were coërced into participating in the denial of our language. They were led to believe that our language interfered in our education. Teachers told our parents that, if we spoke our language, we would have difficulty in school.

Kiciwamanawak, we can do nothing to change the past. Many of my family have never learned our language. But if we are going to share a *Constitution* that protects language, perhaps we can make it easier for them to relearn their language. An elder once told me that when the Cree language was no longer spoken, the wind would stop blowing.

Section 24 of your constitution establishes that "anyone whose rights or freedoms have been infringed may apply to a court of competent jurisdiction for a remedy as the court considers appropriate and just in the circumstances." What happens when I assert that I have a treaty right to my own justice system? Your courts, of whatever jurisdiction, competent or

*Mission School, Lac La Ronge, SK, 1932. My mother attended this school for a year —
long enough to learn to read and write and make a lifelong friend of Beatrice Olson.
(Glenbow Archives, na-4938-35.)*

not, are still your courts. A court of competent jurisdiction would have to be a court established by treaty.

To bring this section into conformity with the treaties, we have to examine the treaty. My family remembers the mutual promises that we would live as before, which included the maintenance of our systems of justice. The law that we agreed to obey and abide by was the law in existence at the time, which was our law, the law of the Creator. We promised to maintain peace and good order between each other. The peace and good order that we promised to keep was the peace and good order that flowed from our obedience and adherence to the law of the Creator. We promised to aid and assist the officers of Her Majesty. I assume this promise is mutual, and requires the officers of Her Majesty to aid and assist us in enforcing the laws in force in the country so shared.

To bring section 24 into conformity with the treaties requires the recognition of my family's justice systems. It also requires that your family and mine aid and assist each other to provide such remedy as appropriate and just in the circumstances. We will have to establish a justice system consistent with treaty that would have jurisdiction to determine rights and freedoms. This justice system would have to be conducted in both our families' languages.

Section 25 of your *Constitution* purports to preserve the rights of my family from the provisions of the *Constitution*. This section takes the treaties out of the *Constitution* and provides that the *Constitution* does not override the treaties. To this extent, the section is consistent with the treaties. Your *Constitution* depends on the treaties for its legitimacy and cannot affect the treaties or any rights or obligations that flow from them. However, underlying this section is the assumption that my family derives rights from your family. The section purports to preserve those rights recognized by the Royal Proclamation. To the extent that the Royal Proclamation of October 7th, 1763, simply recognized that my family had rights, the section needs no modification. Your family can recognize that my family has rights. This recognition in no way infers that those rights are derived from the Royal Proclamation. The Royal Proclamation was not a grant of right; it was simply recognition by your family's monarch that my family has rights.

In subsection (b) of section 25, your *Constitution* purports to preserve "any rights or freedoms that now exist by way of land claims agreements or may be so acquired." This subsection requires modification to make it consistent with the treaties. My family's rights flow from our connection with creation. They are not grants from your family. They cannot be "acquired" through land claims or any other judicial process of your family. Your family's *Constitution* can recognize that my family has rights that cannot be abrogated or derogated. But it cannot be the source of my family's right. *Kiciwamanawak*, my family's rights do not come from you. Your rights come from treaty with my family. Your family needs to protect any rights or freedoms that now exist by way of land claims agreements or may be so acquired. This section of the *Constitution* is written backwards: it is your family that derives rights from treaty.

Section 26 preserves all other rights that were in existence in 1982. This section begs the question of whether a right exists before it is recognized. Does a right to fresh air exist before your family's courts recognize it, or does it come into existence upon recognition?

Section 27 provides that your *Constitution* "shall be interpreted in a manner consistent with the preservation and enhancement of the multi-cultural heritage of Canadians." Let us be certain that there is no confusion here, *Kiciwamanawak*. My family are not the same as other minority groups within your family. We are happy that many people from different parts of the world have come to live here. They are as welcome as you are.

My family adopted your family at treaty. We did not adopt or make treaty with those who are now minorities within your family. To my family, the minorities are all members of your family. They are your responsibility. You adopted them through your ceremony of immigration and naturalization. To the extent that they are your relatives through adoption, they are also our relatives, because you and I are related.

Your family has developed a huge body of law in relation to minorities. You have sought to find peace among yourselves. If my family accepts designation as a minority group, then we would put ourselves under that body of law. I am not in any way criticizing your treatment of minorities, *Kiciwamanawak*. I am simply stating that my family has a different relationship with you. We have a treaty relationship. Our differences must be worked out in accordance with the treaties and not through your law in relation to minorities.

Section 28 of your *Constitution* guarantees rights and freedoms equally to male and female persons. We encourage you to continue down this path of balance.

Section 29 guarantees the rights of certain schools that were protected in the *British North America Act* of 1867. Section 30 extends your *Constitution* to include the Yukon and Northwest Territories. Section 31 clarifies that this *Constitution* does not extend any legislative powers. It does not grant any additional powers to any level of government. These sections do not conflict with the treaties, as far as I can see.

Section 32 limits the application of the *Constitution* to the governments of Canada and the provinces. This section is consistent with the treaties because it does not include my family. This section makes it clear that this *Constitution* applies only to your family's governments. If we are to have a joint constitution under treaty, then this section will have to be modified to include my family's governments.

Section 33 is the "notwithstanding clause." It provides that the governments of Canada or the provinces can expressly take away those rights found in Section 2 and in Sections 7 to 15 of this *Constitution*. How your family gives and takes rights away from your family is none of my concern. But this section cannot be used to take away my family's rights. Despite the protections written into this section, the people who wrote it assumed the supremacy of your governments over all inhabitants of this territory. To bring this section into conformity with the treaties requires that the section include a provision that recognizes that your family received its legitimacy to occupy this territory from the treaties.

Section 34 merely determines the end of that part of the *Constitution Act, 1982* that makes up the *Canadian Charter of Rights and Freedoms*. The following part is not included in the *Charter*. Whether a section is or is not in that portion of the *Constitution* that forms the *Charter* makes little difference to our analysis. Your judges are expected to differentiate between the parts when interpreting the *Constitution*. Their primary consideration would likely be that Section 1, which provides for a balancing of law and rights and freedoms, does not apply to the other parts.

Part II of the *Constitution* of 1982 entitled "Rights of the Aboriginal Peoples of Canada" begins at Section 35, as follows:

(1) The existing Aboriginal and Treaty rights of the Aboriginal peoples of Canada are hereby recognized and affirmed.

(2) In this *Act*, "Aboriginal peoples of Canada" includes the Indian, Inuit and Métis peoples of Canada.

(3) For greater certainty, in subsection (1) "Treaty rights" includes rights that now exist by way of land claims agreements or may be so acquired.

(4) Notwithstanding any other provision of this *Act*, the Aboriginal and Treaty rights referred to in subsection (1) are guaranteed equally to male and female persons.

The drafters of subsection (1) assumed that they could determine Aboriginal and treaty rights. The insertion of the word "existing" was an attempt to limit my family's rights to those deemed as existing in 1982. The assumption was that all rights that had been taken away by your family up to that point would be forever lost. *Kiciwamanawak*, this is backward thinking. Your family cannot determine my family's rights. Our rights do not come from you. Your rights come from treaty. Our rights come from our connection to creation.

This section requires doublethink. First, it assumes that your family can alter the rights of my family, then it purports to "recognize" Aboriginal and treaty rights. If what the drafters intended was to recognize my family as Aboriginal, as the original inhabitants of this territory, then the section is in conformity with the treaties. However, when the drafters attempt to "affirm," as in to "make valid and binding by a formal legal act," they again assume that they have the power to grant rights.

In effect, what this section says is that your family recognizes that my family was here first, and that we have rights. It then states that, even though your family has taken many of those rights away, you will not do that any more. The section recognizes and affirms only those rights that your family has not taken away. It is nothing more than a written promise not to take away rights in the future, with the proviso that everything that has been stolen up to this point is yours.

Here is the doublethink. Section 35 purports to recognize that my family has rights, then purports to give us those rights that we already have. The drafters do not state where their authority to grant and deny a right comes from.

The assumption that your family can determine the rights of my family is never clearly articulated in your constitutional documents. Neither have your courts ever articulated a legitimate theory. Authority is merely assumed. *Kiciwamanawak*, I can only suspect the reason that the theory of your domination is never articulated is because your family does not have one. The old theories of discovery or conquest or emptiness no longer hold true.

We are left trying to make sense of documents and judges' decisions that are based on assumptions of your family's superiority. As soon as we begin to assume equality, those documents and decisions become contorted and nonsensical. As soon as we accept that the treaties were not grants of right from your family, but grants of right to your family, we have to re-decipher all the old judgements and documents that are based on the assumption that your family gave rights to mine.

Not only does your family's historical assumption of superiority diminish my family's rights; it precludes your family's benefiting from the rights obtained at treaty. Since my family adopted yours, your family has the right to occupy and use this territory, but as long as your judges and legislators continue to rely on their assumption of superiority, you have no legitimate right to occupy and use this territory. Not until you accept that we are equal, that we are relatives, can you justify your place in this territory. Superiority has no legitimacy.

Subsection (2) of Section 35 is also inconsistent with the treaties because of its underlying assumption. This subsection purports to determine the Aboriginal peoples of Canada as the Indian, Inuit, and Métis peoples. *Kiciwamanawak*, you haven't the right to tell anyone who they are. It is not for you to decide who is or is not an Indian, who is or is not a member of my family.

Consistent with the assumption underlying subsection (2), your family has enacted legislation in the *Indian Act* that directly determines the limits of my family.[51] The limits in the *Indian Act* are based on assumptions peculiar to your family's way of determining relationships. Elders within my family are afraid that if your determinations are allowed to continue, within a very few generations there will no longer be anyone who meets your requirements to belong to my family. If we allow you to continue to say who is or is not in our family, our family will disappear.

Kiciwamanawak, what do you suppose happens to those of us that your family no longer recognize as Indians? Do we automatically become part of your family? Do we automatically become part of the Métis family? Has anyone asked the Métis whether they accept us? No one has asked us whether we are Indian or Métis or members of your family.

An Aboriginal is a person whose family is Aboriginal. Your laws cannot interfere in that relationship. You cannot come between a mother and her children. Those bonds are sacred. A person in my family may choose to go and live in your family. That is okay. It is a matter of choice. If your family accepts that person, then that person becomes a member of your family. You can use your laws of immigration and naturalization to determine the process of your family's acceptance. That is up to you. The same is true if a member of your family desires to come and live with us. If my family accepts that person, takes them in, adopts them, then they become one of us, a close relative. Our laws of family will determine acceptance or denial.

Subsection (3) of Section 35 is also inconsistent with the treaties because underlying it is the assumption that my family can "acquire" rights from your family. This subsection would be better worded to say, "For greater certainty, 'treaty rights' includes rights to both families that now exist or may be restored through land-sharing agreements."

Subsection (4) of Section 35 recognizes the balance between men and woman and is consistent with the treaties and the Creator's law under which that adoption occurred.

Section 35.1 of your *Constitution* states that, before your family changes its *Constitution* with regard to my family, the prime minister will invite representatives of my family to participate in the discussions. Thank you, *Kiciwamanawak*, but it is not necessary to invite us to talk about your *Con-*

stitution. Only if we accept that you are superior to us and that your *Constitution* determines our existence as a family do we have any right to discuss how your family runs itself. If, however, you want to discuss how the treaties form the basis of your legitimate occupation and use of this territory and how our two families will co-exist in this territory, then I am certain that my family would be happy to carry on lengthy and open discussions.

Section 36 of your *Constitution* provides a commitment between your provincial and federal governments to promote economic development and provide essential public services. The Government of Canada commits to the principle of making equalization payments to the provinces to pay for public services. Section 37 provides for constitutional conferences. Sections 38 to 49 set out the procedure your family will use to amend the *Constitution*. If my family is to be included in the *Constitution*, then my family will have to be included in the provisions for altering the constitution.

Sections 50 and 51 amend the *British North America Act*.

Section 52 states: "The *Constitution* of Canada is the supreme law of Canada, and any law that is inconsistent with the provisions of the *Constitution* is, to the extent of the inconsistency, of no force or effect."

Kiciwamanawak, your *Constitution* is only how your family will run itself. It is not the supreme law of this territory. Your *Constitution* is subservient to and dependent on the treaties for its legitimacy. There is no other legitimate basis for your occupation and use of this territory. It is only by treaty that you have any rights here at all.

You cannot claim to be supreme any longer. You cannot have supreme laws. We are equal. Only when you accept that we are equal, only when you put away your supremacist ideology, can you have any legitimacy. Assertions of supremacy are no longer acceptable. They never were. You are not superior because someone in your family wrote something on a piece of paper and you all agreed that piece of paper and the words written on it were to be your monarch. *Kiciwamanawak*, you do not need to formulate abstract concepts of supremacy for your existence. You have a legitimate claim to this territory. You have treaty rights.

If there is any supreme law, it must be the law of adoption. If your family and mine are going to live in this territory together, with truth and honesty, we have to live as relatives. Sorry, *Kiciwamanawak*, you're stuck with me.

I am not going away. I am not going to disappear or transform into you. Our two families are bound by the ceremony of adoption and we can do nothing to change it. We are forever related "as long as the Sun shines, the Grass grows, and the River flows."

CHAPTER THIRTEEN

Youth

———

Kiciwamanawak, YOUR CRIMINAL JUSTICE people — the police, judges, and prosecutors — participate in locking up far too many of my family's youth. Your family has prepared statistics that indicate most of these young people are in jail for property offences. Even when we look at offences against the person, a large percentage are robbery, which is in effect a property offence.

Your family has long recognized that there is a direct connection between poverty and crime. Your family has also recognized, at least since the treaties, my family's poverty. My nephews and nieces are in your jails because they are poor. They commit what your family calls a crime because they do not have enough.

When the people in this province's government are asked why they have so many young people in jail, they respond by saying it is because there are high numbers of Aboriginal people in this territory. If we ask, "Do you lock them up because they are Aboriginal?" they will say, "No, it is because Aboriginal youth commit more crimes." We can, at this point, expect to hear statistical excuses that link poverty, education, and social and economic factors to crime. Then we have to ask, "Do you lock us up because we are poor?"

Why are we poor? Is it because your family denies us access to the wealth and bounty of our Mother? Are we poor because your family insists on its superiority? Are we poor because the extraction of wealth is reserved for the wealthy?

In many cases, your jails offer better living conditions than my family experiences at home — if we have a home. In jail we are assured of food, shelter, clothing, and family. In jail we receive three meals a day. We do not have to sleep on the street, or on the floor, or in an overcrowded slum. We do not have to worry whether we have warm winter clothing, and we can be sure to meet our relatives there. *Kiciwamanawak* forms the majority. *Kiciwamanawak*, is _____ to alleviate our poverty? *Kiciwamanawak* _____ have a problem with the people who work within _____ that sends our children to jail. The structures these people work within are a "jail-stream." Your government has enacted the *Youth Criminal Justice Act*, which satisfies those of your family who were screaming for harsher punishment for children. They made an incredible noise about young people committing murder and only receiving three-year prison sentences. The *Act* allows youth who have committed serious violent acts to be more easily moved into the adult system. This part of the *Act* speeds up the jail-stream that was always there.

The other part of the *Act* mandates that children who have not committed a violent crime not be sent to jail. Taken in isolation, this part of the *Act* appears to remedy the problem of over-incarceration of youth. Canada locks up more children than any other industrialized country in the world. Saskatchewan locks up more children than anywhere else in Canada, and northern Saskatchewan locks up more children than the rest of the province.

The over-use of incarceration has been a serious problem in the north for a long time. The problem is that the people who _____ the courts have not had any options. In the north _____ to incarceration. The provincial government _____ resources into northern communities _____ A judge faced with an offender must fashion _____ offence. When there are no community resources, the judge's options are limited to sending the child to a southern institution.

The *Act* will not slow the jail-stream. Legislation on its own rarely solves problems. The same problems exist after the passage of the legislation as existed before. Northern communities do not have the resources to provide alternatives to custodial sentences. Our children are sent away to southern institutions to learn how to become better criminals. The northern communities not only have no resources to prevent the jail-stream, but they have no resources to deal with the new wave of crime imported from southern jails.

Today, in this territory, my nephews and nieces are joining gangs. I understand that this causes fear and uncertainty for your family. These young people should not be feared. They are merely showing us that they need to belong — to a family, to a community, and to a nation. They need to be respected and accepted. If the larger society cannot meet their needs, they will form gangs that do. Instead of trying to eradicate the gangs, we might learn how a gang creates and maintains family and community.

Assimilation of my family has not resulted in us becoming you. What has occurred is that many of my family's youth no longer have an Aboriginal identity. They do not have our tradition or our ceremonies. They have not been told the stories that hold our history and our knowledge. At the same time, they have not adopted your social structures, your traditions, and your ceremonies. They are cultural blanks. These youth will create their own culture, borrowing from others. They borrow from the African American culture that they see on television. They borrow from the street culture they found on migration from the reserves to city ghettos. This new culture will not accept your family's domination, will not accept your values, and will not accept your worldview. They remain Indian, but do not know what it means to be Indian. All your assimilation efforts have failed, and now you and I are responsible for the consequences.

Our youth do not respect your institutions and they do not know their own. For many of today's youth, a criminal record is a badge of honour, something to be proud of. Your criminal justice system begins sanctions against children as young as 12. These are children just past the age of innocence. They have not yet learned of choice and consequence. They are still playing.

In my family's understanding, a person is innocent during the first seven years. They are not yet even completely of this world; they still have connections with the spirit world from where they recently came. During the next seven years they are children, from about seven to fourteen, just learning to be in this world. It is a time of learning through play. The next seven years they learn about the world and their place in it. We have ceremonies to help these people through the stages. The becoming a man and becoming a woman ceremony are vital to their development and to their spiritual alignment in this world. The ceremonies integrate the youth in this world with their families, their community, and their nation. They also integrate the youth with the spirit world so that the youth walks in balance.

This is the age, from 14 to 21, when young persons traditionally sought their vision through fasting and prayer. Their vision, uniquely their own, set the path for their life. The remainder of their life should be a walk toward that vision. Assimilation policy and practice has disrupted this traditional progression. Today, most youth have not integrated into any society beyond their own making. They wander this world without guidance from the spirit world. They have no vision for their life. This is a time when they should be learning choice and consequence, a time to experience themselves within this world.

Some of these youth have fetal alcohol syndrome. In the city ghettos, we are now experiencing fetal alcohol syndrome children giving birth to fetal solvent syndrome babies. What are we going to do with the next generation of broken children? Who is going to take responsibility? Who is going to stop the retailers from selling solvents to the children?

My nieces are selling themselves to people on the street. These girls are little more than babies. They have only recently passed from the age of innocence to the back seats of pedophiles' cars. A police officer once told me that a twelve-year-old girl had offered to do whatever he wanted for as long as he wanted, if only he would give her enough money to buy a pair of brand-name running shoes.

CHAPTER FOURTEEN

Next Generations

AT THIS PIVOTAL MOMENT, we are at the time of greatest change in all the history of humankind. Your family's understanding of the physical universe doubled once between the time of Christ and 1,000 C.E. Between 1,000 C.E. and the time your family arrived on the shore of Turtle Island, your understanding of the physical universe doubled again. Between that moment of contact and the beginning of your industrial revolution, your understanding doubled again. Each doubling of your understanding took half the amount of time of the previous one. The last doubling I heard of took about 18 months. Will the next doubling occur in nine months, four and a half months, two months, one month, two weeks? Is it possible that within the next few years knowledge of the physical universe will be doubling every minute?

Now we must look to the future and try to imagine seven generations ahead. *Kiciwamanawak*, the future is ours to create. Choices that we make in this moment will have consequences for our children, our grandchildren, our great grandchildren, and so on. This insight is not unique to my family. It is a teaching also of the Christian, Muslim, and Hebrew faiths. The books of Moses in the Bible, in the Torah, and in the Qur'an tell of God's wrath against the next four generations of an evildoer. We knew long before your missionaries arrived here to project at least seven generations ahead.

Any look toward the future must begin in this pivotal moment. There is not much we can do to change our situation, *Kiciwamanawak*. You and I are too old to change now, or so we like to say. Yet we must. We must find the courage to change so that future generations have a chance. We must follow our vision boldly and faithfully. The future will be whatever we imagine it to be. But without a vision we will continue to make the same mistakes and wallow in our present sorrow.

From my own experience, I have learned that I cannot do anything until I can imagine doing it. As a youth, I was able to imagine joining the Canadian Armed Forces because a man in my community came home in uniform. On release from the Armed Forces, I was able to imagine myself as a journeyman mechanic, and sought to continue in that trade. I was able to imagine myself a logger and a miner and a heavy equipment operator because my brothers had worked in those trades. I was able to imagine myself as a trapper and a fisherman because those were the trades of my father. By chance, I met a man who helped me imagine that I could become a lawyer. In law school I met a professor who helped me imagine that I could intern for the International Labour Organization in Geneva, Switzerland. Another professor helped me imagine that I could go to Harvard Law School for a master's degree. Today I imagine living close to the earth and using the gifts and blessings of my grandfathers and grandmothers to help create a more tolerant world for the next generations, so that they might experience good health and happiness.

Kiciwamanawak, we can help others to imagine their own visions and support them as they walk toward them. We can take down the barriers that limit imagination and open up space within our structures for imagination. We can critically examine the existing structures to find where they limit imagination and where they create unnecessary shortages, where they waste resources and energy.

Self-government cannot be imposed by your family on mine. Whatever form of home rule my family adopts must come from our own collective imagination. The form of band government that we now experience comes from your *Indian Act*. This form of government is inadequate to deal with all the problems caused by the imposition of the *Act*.

The band government structure imposed on us requires resources and energy to maintain it. Band councils and chiefs and support staff are kept busy maintaining the structure. They are required to hold expensive elections that take even more energy and resources. This foreign style of leadership selection also imports adversarialism and animosity into our communities. Too much time, energy, and resources are spent maintaining the structure of government, which takes away from the amount available for the work of government.

The same situation is found off reserve. Community organizations are required to abide by the structures imposed by the *Non-Profit Incorporation Acts* in each province. These *Acts* impose expensive structures on people who are trying to assist my family members. The meagre resources that a non-government organization can acquire are taken up by the requirements of legislation. Often, on reserve and off, a band council or a non-government organization faced with inadequate resources will opt to use those resources to assist people in priority over structural maintenance.

Fort Pitt, Saskatchewan, 1884. From the left: Four Sky Thunder, Sky Bird (or King Bird), Matoose (seated), Naposis, Big Bear, Anguys McKay, Mr. Dufresne, Louis Goulet, Stanley Simpson, Constable G. W. Rowley (seated), and Alex McDonald (in back). King Bird was the third son of Big Bear. (Glenbow Archives, na-1323-4.)

When this occurs, they breach the structural requirements and become discredited as non-democratic.

Kiciwamanawak, your imposed forms of government are too expensive for my family. They limit our ability to assist ourselves. While we learn your reporting requirements, hold elections, fill in the forms, write progress reports, create and maintain master/servant relationships with the workers, and defend our credibility, the work that we hope to achieve goes undone. Can you imagine people working with only enough structure to ensure that the work gets done? Can you imagine healthy, balanced people assisting each other without a master, without being servants?

There are several ways that we can share the resources. Your family can continue to be the main extractor and use your corporations as vehicles for extraction. You would then give my family a share based on our population — not a share of the royalties your governments collect from the corporations but a share of the resources that are extracted. We will in the near future be 20 per cent of this territory's population. So we would receive 20 percent of all timber, uranium, potash, oil, and gas.

Or we can agree that 20 per cent of all resources in the territory can only be extracted by my family. My family will then form its own vehicles to extract those resources. Your family will not interfere in how we extract the resources or whom we sell them to or how much we sell them for. If we chose to harvest timber with horses and maximize employment, or if we chose to harvest with mechanical harvesters and maximize profits for a few, will be our choice. Likewise, if we chose to selectively log and preserve our Mother, or whether we cut and slash and clear-cut, will be our choice. We will live with the consequences of our choice. I have faith that my family will make wise choices concerning our Mother. But whatever the choice, it has to be ours.

Kiciwamanawak, can you imagine not interfering in my family's hunting, fishing, gathering, and trapping? Can you imagine leaving that entirely up to us? You can continue to live like before. You can raise beef, grow grain, keep your farms. My family will not interfere. But you leave all the ' wildlife under our care and management. Very little will likely change with regard to your family's hunting for sport, except that the sports hunters would have to purchase a licence from my family. Your family does not need to hunt for food. Your hunters are primarily interested in sport, in trophy hunting. The way things are set up now, these trophy hunters have political power through their Wildlife Federation, and they can influence your government with regard to hunting regulations. Of course, they influence things in their favour. Ontario and British Columbia have already passed legislation that elevates sports hunting and fishing to rights, while the proposed *Heritage Hunting and Fishing Act*, a federal Private Member's Bill, aims at the same thing on a broader basis.[52]

My family continues to survive by hunting and fishing and trapping and gathering. Wildlife continues to be a primary source of food for many of my relatives. Even though trapping and fishing no longer provide an acceptable standard of living, these pursuits continue to subsidize many of my family members' income. We still have that connection to our Mother.

I anticipate that, if we are to assist my nephews and nieces who live in your city ghettos, we will have to reintegrate them with their culture, their food, their tradition, and with their Mother the Earth. Hunting, fishing, trapping, and gathering are a means to this reintegration. My family needs to be able to exercise these pursuits without interference. *Kiciwamanawak*, we need you to live up to the promises your family made at treaty not to interfere.

Kiciwamanawak, any look to the future will have to examine globalization. Globalization is set to shape the world into one unit without borders, in which will govern a dictatorship of powerful commercial banks and multinational corporations. We will not have to argue between us about sovereignty, *Kiciwamanawak*. We will both bow to the dictates of people outside this territory. My family cannot protect itself from globalization. Neither can it participate while we are dominated by your family.

It is possible that, if my family gains access to resources, we might create enclaves of co-operation and mutual support that will be resistant to globalization. If we follow our tradition of respect for the earth, of co-operation and self-sufficiency, the global agenda of integrated markets might have nothing to offer us. It might be too late, though. My family might be seduced by the promise of plenty and sell our inheritance for a moment of pleasure along with your family. We are human. We are as capable of making mistakes as you are, *Kiciwamanawak*.

Kiciwamanawak, we cannot depend on government or the mythical "them" to solve our problems. You and I are the experts. Only we know what is in our hearts, in our minds. Only we know our visions, our hopes, and our dreams of a better future for the generations to come. My family cannot leave things up to the Assembly of First Nations or the Federation of Saskatchewan Indian Nations. The people appointed to work within these structures are good people. They work within the confines of the structures to better the lives of my family. But, like everyone else within a structure, they are limited by the structure and the requirement to maintain it. Their energy and resources are further sapped by their attempts to interact with your structures of Indian Affairs, Justice, Health, and Education. Just the fact that your government people work in silos with strict boundaries requires that we expend our meagre resources in duplicate forums.

Kiciwamanawak, my family has created structures — FSIN, AFN — to interact with your structures. Our present government structure is a reaction to your government structures. It is also dictated by your structures. The *Indian Act* details how the chief and council of each First Nation is elected and dictates their powers. Much of a chief's and council's work revolves around the reporting requirements of your government. If the only way my family can communicate with your family is through parallel structures, we will never be able to resolve the differences between us. We need to meet as humans and put aside ideas of superiority so that we can work together toward a better future.

It might be difficult to imagine not having structures. How will you provide for your needs if you remove structure? After all, the structures provide you with employment. If it were not for the structures, how would you provide for yourselves? These are honest questions. But they are not questions about the future as much as they are restatements of our shared past. We have become dependent on the structures, and, from within the structures, we cannot imagine life outside. Our vision has become limited. We do have needs that must be satisfied — the basic needs of food, shelter, and clothing, along with our need to belong and to be a part of family and community. At present, the structures tend to provide for the first set of needs — food, shelter, and clothing, the basic needs — but they interfere with the other needs of belonging. The structures tend to place us in isolated boxes, and condemn us to competition with others.

We can best provide for our basic needs through co-operation and at the same time strengthen our connections to family and community. *Kiciwamanawak*, you do not have to change your structures, your way of being. All that my family asks is that you stop imposing your way of being on us. Give my family the room to re-establish our families and communities. Stop restricting our access to the resources of our Mother. Stop imposing your structures of justice and health and social services and education.

My family has survived here since the Creator placed us here. The Earth our Mother continues to provide her bounty. This is a rich territory where both our families can meet all our needs. The reason my family lives in perpetual poverty is not that there are not enough resources, but because we are restricted and regulated and have become dependent on your structures for our very survival.

If we are to have a vision of the future, *Kiciwamanawak*, the vision must be one that provides for our children and grandchildren and great grandchildren. This should be a vision that has at its end freedom from tyranny. The steps toward that vision will be small and deliberate. As your family withdraws its tyrannical order, my family will learn independence. We will then return to the law of our Creator and make our choices knowing that we will live with the consequences. I assure you, *Kiciwamanawak*, that my family can provide for its needs if we are allowed access to the shared territory as was agreed in the treaties between your ancestors and mine. The vision for the future available to us in this moment includes the vision of our ancestors. In truth, we are not creating a new vision, but re-envisioning the treaties and keeping those perpetual promises.

There is another fear, *Kiciwamanawak*. This is the need for security. We have been taught that, without tyranny, we would become murderers and thieves. We have been taught that, without our benevolent tyrants, we would be in a constant state of warfare. We have believed these lies about ourselves and have clung to our tyrants for protection from ourselves. The tyrants tell us that the others in our families would attack us if the tyrants did not keep them in order. The tyrants tell the others that you and I would attack them if the tyrants did not keep us in order. These are lies. Both you and I know, *Kiciwamanawak*, deep within ourselves, that we would attack no one if we were allowed to live in peace.

There is no evidence to support these lies, *Kiciwamanawak*. Nowhere has there been the mad destruction and violence predicted by our tyrants when there were no tyrants. All the wars and violence that have occurred have been the result of clashes between tyrants or the overthrow of tyrants. People left to their own have never become violent and destructive.

The evidence of this territory indicates that tyranny does not keep order. When tyranny is imposed on peaceful people, they become violent and disorderly. In the northern communities, there was very little crime of any sort until the RCMP arrived. In isolated communities, the people kept order among themselves based on respect. When roads, the RCMP, and bootleggers arrived — usually simultaneously — order broke down. People surrendered their personal authority to the RCMP. Crime rates increased because individuals were no longer responsible for community peace. That responsibility was surrendered to people not of the community, and therefore not deserving of respect.

Ultimately, *Kiciwamanawak*, order is up to us. Your people who work within the justice system are beginning to recognize communities have to be involved, and that the system as a stand-alone system has failed. Community justice committees are now being asked to find the solutions that the tyrants could not. We are beyond the day of arrogance. No longer do people respect tyranny. Slowly the people who work within the justice system are beginning to recognize that a uniform or a judicial robe does not automatically garner respect.

The justice system within your family has been amazing to watch. The more it fails, the more money you pour into it. The more the professionals within the system are unable to find solutions, the more they are rewarded. The more disorder results from the justice system, the more it is supported. The more destruction and violence the system causes, the more time and money and effort are poured into it.

Kiciwamanawak, there is more than fear that keeps tyranny in place. There are also the many individuals within the structures who depend on their positions of prestige and power. These people are not going to willingly accept that they are human. Many of them have believed for their entire lives that they are more god-like than human. Their belief in their superiority will be difficult for them to let go of.

Our vision for the future can exclude these non-humans. They are non-humans because all humans are equal and these people believe they are superior. In their drunkenness, they have illusions that they are gods: the illusion creates the drunkenness and is created by the drunkenness. They believe in their superiority and, in acting on that belief, are rewarded within the structures that they create based upon the belief. It is a cycle of drunkenness and power and power and drunkenness.

Kiciwamanawak, there are no superior beings. We are all human. We are all blessed with the ability to make choices and to learn from the consequences of those choices. Theorists have used the fact that we are human against us to keep us from achieving a better world. The argument against utopia is that it is unachievable and therefore not worth attempting. I agree that utopia is unachievable, but that should not stop us from seeking it. Only by seeking the impossible can we go beyond our self-imposed limits. Utopia is that state of human organization in which we achieve perfect peace and harmony. It is unachievable because we are imperfect humans. Only perfect humans or gods can live in utopia.

Kiciwamanawak, my understanding of my place in this world, as explained to me by an elder, is that I was a spirit travelling through the universe and sought to be closer to the Creator. To get closer to the Creator, I had to experience the physical world because the Creator is both physical and spiritual. My time on this earth is to be spent seeking my Creator. To fulfill my purpose here, I should keep the Creator in my mind at all times and seek through experience the perfection of the Creator expressed in creation. In seeking the Creator, I should never allow another to come between. I should put no humans above me.

It is also a teaching of my family that only a human will deceive you. Our relatives the animals and plants and those in the spirit world will never lie to us. Only humans are deceptive, and we are advised never to put our faith in another human if we do not want to experience disappointment. Utopia is unachievable in this world. We have to accept that we are human and everyone else around us is likewise human. Once we accept this basic truth, we can begin to seek perfection. We might never be able to achieve the utopia of the gods, but we can seek the human equivalent, a human utopia, or, to create a new word, a hutopia.

My family has lived for thousands of years in this territory. Our stories, our oral history, tell of living in harmony with all creation. Our stories tell us that we are relatives to the plants and animals, that our ancestors are a part of the cycle. They died, their bodies decayed and went back into the earth and were eaten by the animals that we eat today. Our ancestors are a part of us. We are connected to all living things within this territory. We had societies based on this understanding. These were societies that were tolerant and accepting of human error.

I understand your family, *Kiciwamanawak,* have a different understanding of human nature. You use the failings of humans as an excuse for superiority. Your élite justify their positions by pointing out the failings of the masses. They do not admit their own failings, their own humanness. This has been a part of your family for so long that now it is unquestioned. We are not concerned that your family organizes itself according to superiority concepts. That is your way. It works for you. The problem is when that ideology is imposed on the rest of the world. Not only does your family adhere to the ideology within your family; it tends to propagate the ideology universally.

The idea of superiority is the cornerstone of your created structures, and those structures have a symbiotic relationship with the ideology. The structures are created by the ideology and maintain the ideology. When the structures are imposed on other families, superiority ideology takes on a new dimension. It becomes the superiority of your family over other families.

Many of your family members now accept that your family is the greatest in all of history. It will take a long time for them to become accepting and tolerant. They seek to do good. But when they approach a problem they tend to try to solve it by relying on superiority ideology. They simply fall back on what they think they know without recognizing the limits of what they know. Teachers, preachers, police officers, and social workers interact with my family daily. Even when these people recognize that the programs and policies that they administer do not work, they are trapped by their structures, their governing legislation, their board policy, their constitutions, hierarchies, and departmentalization. The structures prevent them from finding workable solutions. Even if these individuals do not believe your family is superior to mine, they are limited by the superiority ideology inherent in their structures.

Kiciwamanawak, our future is ours to determine. You alone have the responsibility for the future generations. Your choices will determine the life of our children and grandchildren and their grandchildren. You have incredible power. You have the power of choice. Do not accept that you are inconsequential. The Creator made each of us with a purpose, a high purpose. It is for us to accept our responsibilities and reach for our ultimate potential. Now that you know that the artificial structures of your family have no power over you, you are as free as my family. The choice is yours.

I have become convinced that my family will not be freed from tyranny until your family members free their minds from tyranny. Not until the dominant culture ceases to assume that its structures are natural, necessary, and superior will it cease to impose its ideology over my family. Your family's domination must end. My family's survival as Indians depends on your family's leaving us room to be Indians, to be independent and self-sufficient.

Kiciwamanawak, I am not suggesting that you revolt against your family. I am not suggesting an armed rebellion. Nor am I suggesting that you overthrow your government. The structures of your family are your family's structures. They belong to you. I expect that you will remain loyal to your family and even loyal to the structures that your family has created. All I am asking is that you recognize that they are created structures and that they have been created pursuant to superiority ideology. I am not telling you what to do. I am not interfering in your life, in your family.

I am offering a solution to the very serious problems that I see in this territory. If we return to the original intention of treaty and recognize that we are relatives, *Kiciwamanawak,* we should be able to walk into the future in a good way.

Treaty No. 6

ARTICLES OF A TREATY made and concluded near Carlton on the 23rd day of August and on the 28th day of said month, respectively, and near Fort Pitt on the 9th day of September, in the year of Our Lord one thousand eight hundred and seventy-six, between Her Most Gracious Majesty the Queen of Great Britain and Ireland, by Her Commissioners, the Honourable Alexander Morris, Lieutenant-Governor of the Province of Manitoba and the North-West Territories, and the Honourable James McKay, and the Honourable William Joseph Christie, of the one part, and the Plain and Wood Cree and the other Tribes of Indians, inhabitants of the country within the limits hereinafter defined and described by their Chiefs, chosen and named as hereinafter mentioned, of the other part.

Whereas the Indians inhabiting the said country have, pursuant to an appointment made by the said Commissioners, been convened at meetings at Fort Carlton, Fort Pitt and Battle River, to deliberate upon certain matters of interest to Her Most Gracious Majesty, of the one part, and the said Indians of the other.

And whereas the said Indians have been notified and informed by Her Majesty's said Commissioners that it is the desire of Her Majesty to open up for settlement, immigration and such other purposes as to Her Majesty may seem meet, a tract of country bounded and described as hereinafter mentioned, and to obtain the consent thereto of Her Indian subjects inhabiting the said tract, and to make a treaty and arrange with them, so that there may be peace and good will between them and Her Majesty, and that they may know and be assured of what allowance they are to count upon and receive from Her Majesty's bounty and benevolence.

And whereas the Indians of the said tract, duly convened in council, as aforesaid, and being requested by Her Majesty's said Commissioners to name certain Chiefs and Headmen, who should be authorized on their behalf to conduct such negotiations and sign any treaty to be founded thereon, and to become responsible to Her Majesty for their faithful performance by their respective Bands of such obligations as shall be assumed by them, the said Indians have thereupon named for that purpose, that is to say, representing the Indians who make the treaty at Carlton, the several Chiefs and Councillors who have subscribed hereto, and representing the Indians who make the treaty at Fort Pitt, the several Chiefs and Councillors who have subscribed hereto.

And thereupon, in open council, the different Bands having presented their Chiefs to the said Commissioners as the Chiefs and Headmen, for the purposes aforesaid, of the respective Bands of Indians inhabiting the said district hereinafter described.

And whereas, the said Commissioners then and there received and acknowledged the persons so presented as Chiefs and Headmen, for the purposes aforesaid, of the respective Bands of Indians inhabiting the said district hereinafter described.

And whereas, the said Commissioners have proceeded to negotiate a treaty with the said Indians, and the same has been finally agreed upon and concluded, as follows, that is to say:

The Plain and Wood Cree Tribes of Indians, and all the other Indians inhabiting the district hereinafter described and defined, do hereby cede, release, surrender and yield up to the Government of the Dominion of Canada, for Her Majesty the Queen and Her successors forever, all their rights, titles and privileges, whatsoever, to the lands included within the following limits, that is to say:

Commencing at the mouth of the river emptying into the north-west angle of Cumberland Lake; thence westerly up the said river to its source; thence on a straight line in a westerly direction to the head of Green Lake; thence northerly to the elbow in the Beaver River; thence down the said river northerly to a point twenty miles from the said elbow; thence in a westerly direction, keeping on a line generally parallel with the said Beaver River (above the elbow), and about twenty miles distant therefrom, to the source of the said river; thence northerly to the north-easterly point of the south shore of Red Deer Lake, continuing westerly along the said shore to the western limit thereof; and thence due west to the Athabasca River; thence up the said river, against the stream, to the Jaspar House, in the Rocky Mountains; thence on a course south-easterly, following the easterly range of the mountains, to the source of the main branch of the Red Deer River; thence down the said river, with the stream, to the junction therewith of the outlet of the river, being the outlet of the Buffalo Lake; thence due east twenty miles; thence on a straight line south-eastwardly to the mouth of the said Red Deer River on the south branch of the Saskatchewan River; thence eastwardly and northwardly, following on the boundaries of the tracts conceded by the several treaties numbered four and five to the place of beginning.

And also, all their rights, titles and privileges whatsoever to all other lands wherever situated in the North-West Territories, or in any other Province or portion of Her Majesty's Dominions, situated and being within the Dominion of Canada.

The tract comprised within the lines above described embracing an area of 121,000 square miles, be the same more or less.

To have and to hold the same to Her Majesty the Queen and Her successors forever.

And Her Majesty the Queen hereby agrees and undertakes to lay aside reserves for farming lands, due respect being had to lands at present cultivated by the said Indians, and other reserves for the benefit of the said Indians, to be administered and dealt with for them by Her Majesty's Government of the Dominion of Canada; provided, all such reserves shall not exceed in all one square mile for each family of five, or in that proportion for larger or smaller families, in manner following, that is to say: that the Chief Superintendent of Indian Affairs shall depute and send a suitable person to determine and set apart the reserves for each band, after consulting with the Indians thereof as to the locality which may be found to be most suitable for them.

Provided, however, that Her Majesty reserves the right to deal with any settlers within the bounds of any lands reserved for any Band as She shall deem fit, and also that the aforesaid reserves of land, or any interest therein, may be sold or otherwise disposed of by Her Majesty's Government for the use and benefit of the said Indians entitled thereto, with their consent first had and obtained; and with a view to show the satisfaction of Her Majesty with the behaviour and good conduct of Her Indians, She hereby, through Her Commissioners, makes them a present of twelve dollars for each man, woman and child belonging to the Bands here represented, in extinguishment of all claims heretofore preferred.

And further, Her Majesty agrees to maintain schools for instruction in such reserves hereby made as to Her Government of the Dominion of Canada may seem advisable, whenever the Indians of the reserve shall desire it.

Her Majesty further agrees with Her said Indians that within the boundary of Indian reserves, until otherwise determined by Her Government of the Dominion of Canada, no intoxicating liquor shall be allowed to be introduced or sold, and all laws now in force, or hereafter to be enacted, to preserve Her Indian subjects inhabiting the reserves or living elsewhere within Her North-West Territories from the evil influence of the use of intoxicating liquors, shall be strictly enforced.

Her Majesty further agrees with Her said Indians that they, the said Indians, shall have the right to pursue their avocations of hunting and fishing throughout the tract surrendered as hereinbefore described, subject to such regulations as may from time to time be made by Her Government of Her Dominion of Canada, and saving and excepting such tracts as may from time to time be required or taken up for settlement, mining, lumbering or other purposes by Her said Government of the Dominion of Canada, or by any of the subjects thereof duly authorized therefor by the said Government.

It is further agreed between Her Majesty and Her said Indians, that such sections of the reserves above indicated as may at any time be required for public works or buildings, of what nature soever, may be appropriated for that purpose by Her Majesty's Government of the Dominion of Canada, due compensation being made for the value of any improvements thereon.

And further, that Her Majesty's Commissioners shall, as soon as possible after the execution of this treaty, cause to be taken an accurate census of all the Indians inhabiting the tract above described, distributing them in families, and shall, in every year ensuing the date hereof, at some period in each year, to be duly notified to the Indians, and at a place or places to be appointed for that purpose within the territory ceded, pay to each Indian person the sum of $5 per head yearly.

It is further agreed between Her Majesty and the said Indians, that the sum of $1,500.00 per annum shall be yearly and every year expended by Her Majesty in the purchase of ammunition, and twine for nets, for the use of the said Indians, in manner following, that is to say: In the reasonable discretion, as regards the distribution thereof among the Indians inhabiting the several reserves, or otherwise, included herein, of Her Majesty's Indian Agent having the supervision of this treaty.

It is further agreed between Her Majesty and the said Indians, that the following articles shall be supplied to any Band of the said Indians who are now cultivating the soil, or who shall hereafter commence to cultivate the land, that is to say: Four hoes for every family actually cultivating; also, two spades per family as aforesaid: one plough for every three families, as aforesaid; one harrow for every three families, as aforesaid; two scythes and one whetstone, and two hay forks and two reaping hooks, for every family as aforesaid, and also two axes; and also one cross-cut saw, one hand-saw, one pit-saw, the necessary files, one grindstone and one auger for each Band; and also for each Chief for the use of his Band, one chest of ordinary carpenter's tools; also, for each Band, enough of wheat, barley, potatoes and oats to plant the land actually broken up for cultivation by such Band; also for each Band four oxen, one bull and six cows; also, one boar and two sows, and one hand-mill when any Band shall raise sufficient grain therefor. All the aforesaid articles to be given once and for all for the encouragement of the practice of agriculture among the Indians.

It is further agreed between Her Majesty and the said Indians, that each Chief, duly recognized as such, shall receive an annual salary of twenty-five dollars per annum; and each subordinate officer, not exceeding four for each Band, shall receive fifteen dollars per annum; and each such Chief and subordinate officer, as aforesaid, shall also receive once every year, a suitable suit of clothing, and each Chief shall receive, in recognition of the closing of the treaty, a suitable flag and medal, and also as soon as convenient, one horse, harness and waggon.

That in the event hereafter of the Indians comprised within this treaty being overtaken by any pestilence, or by a general famine, the Queen, on being satisfied and certified thereof by Her Indian Agent or Agents, will grant to the Indians assistance of such character and to such extent as Her Chief Superintendent of Indian Affairs shall deem necessary and sufficient to relieve the Indians from the calamity that shall have befallen them.

That during the next three years, after two or more of the reserves hereby agreed to be set apart to the Indians shall have been agreed upon and surveyed, there shall be granted to the Indians included under the Chiefs adhering to the treaty at Carlton, each spring, the sum of one thousand dollars, to be expended for them by Her Majesty's Indian Agents, in the purchase of provisions for the use of such of the Band as are actually settled on the reserves and are engaged in cultivating the soil, to assist them in such cultivation.

That a medicine chest shall be kept at the house of each Indian Agent for the use and benefit of the Indians at the direction of such agent.

That with regard to the Indians included under the Chiefs adhering to the treaty at Fort Pitt, and to those under Chiefs within the treaty limits who may hereafter give their adhesion thereto (exclusively, however, of the Indians of the Carlton region), there shall, during three years, after two or more reserves shall have been agreed upon and surveyed be distributed each spring among the Bands cultivating the soil on such reserves, by Her Majesty's Chief Indian Agent for this treaty, in his discretion, a sum not exceeding one thousand dollars, in the purchase of provisions for the use of such members of the Band as are actually settled on the reserves and engaged in the cultivation of the soil, to assist and encourage them in such cultivation.

That in lieu of waggons, if they desire it and declare their option to that effect, there shall be given to each of the Chiefs adhering hereto at Fort Pitt or elsewhere hereafter (exclusively of those in the Carlton district), in recognition of this treaty, as soon as the same can be conveniently transported, two carts with iron bushings and tires.

And the undersigned Chiefs on their own behalf and on behalf of all other Indians inhabiting the tract within ceded, do hereby solemnly promise and engage to strictly observe this treaty, and also to conduct and behave themselves as good and loyal subjects of Her Majesty the Queen.

They promise and engage that they will in all respects obey and abide by the law, and they will maintain peace and good order between each other, and also between themselves and other tribes of Indians, and between themselves and others of Her Majesty's subjects, whether Indians or whites, now inhabiting or hereafter to inhabit any part of the said ceded tracts, and that they will not molest the person or property of any inhabitant of such ceded tracts, or the property of Her Majesty the Queen, or interfere with or trouble any person passing or travelling through the said tracts, or any part thereof, and that they will aid and assist the officers of Her Majesty in bringing to justice and punishment any Indian offending against the stipulations of this treaty, or infringing the laws in force in the country so ceded.

In witness whereoff, Her Majesty's said Commissioners and the said Indian Chiefs have hereunto subscribed and set their hands at or near Fort Carlton, on the days and year aforesaid, and near Fort Pitt on the day above aforesaid.

Alexander Morris, L.G., N.W.T.

Indian Commissioners
James McKay
W. J. Christie

Head Chiefs of the Carlton Indians
Mis-to-wa-sis, his mark
Ah-tuk-uk-koop, his mark

Chiefs
Pee-yahn-kah-nihk-oo-sit, his mark
Ah-yah-tus-kum-ik-im-um, his mark
Kee-too-wa-han, his mark
Cha-kas-ta-han, his mark
John Smith, his mark
James Smith, his mark
Chip-ee-way-an, his mark

Councillors of Mis-to-wa-sis
Mass-an, his mark
Pierre Cadien, his mark
Koo-yah-tik-wah-pahn, his mark
Mahs-kee-te-tim-un, his mark

Councillors of Ah-tuk-uk-koop
SAH-SAH-KOO-MOOS, his mark
BENJAMIN, his mark
MEE-NOW-AH-CHAHK-WAY, his mark
KEE-SIK-OW-AS-IS, his mark

Councillors of Pee-yahn-kah-nihk-oo-sit
PEE-TOOK-AH-HAN AP-EE-GIN-EW, his mark
PEE-AY-CHEW, his mark
TAH-WAH-JUSK EE-KAHP-POW, his mark
AHS-KOOS, his mark

Councillors of Kee-too-wa-han
PET-E-QUA-CAY, his mark
JEAN BAPTISTE, his mark
ISADORE WOLFE, his mark
KEE-KOO-HOOS, his mark

Councillors of Ah-yah-tus-kum-ik-im-um
OO-SAHN-ASKU-NUKIP, his mark
YAH-YAW-LOO-WAY, his mark
SOO-SOU-AIM-EE-LUAHN, his mark
NEES-WAH-YAK-EE-NAH-KOOS, his mark

Councillors of Cha-kas-ta-han
KAH-TIP-IS-KOOR-AHT, his mark
KAH-KUN-EE-KWAHW-AHS-UM, his mark
NAH-PACH, his mark
MUS-IN-AH-NE-HIM-AHN, his mark

Councillors of John Smith
WILLIAM BADGER
BENJAMIN JOYFUL, his mark
JOHN BADGER
JAMES BEAR
BERNARD CONSTANT

Councillors of James Smith
HENRY SMITH, his mark
MAH-TWA-AHS-TIM-OO-WE-GIN, his mark
JACOB McLEAN, his mark

Councillors of Chip-ee-way-an
NAA-POO-CHEE-CHEES, his mark
WAH-WIS, his mark
KAH-PAH-PAH-MAH-CHATIK-WAY, his mark
KEE-YEU-AH-TEA-PEM-WAHT, his mark

Signed by the Chiefs within named in presence of the following witnesses, the same having been first read and explained by Peter Erasmus, Peter Ballendine and the Rev. John McKay:

ALF JACKES, M.D.
JAS. WALKER, N.W.M.P.
J. H. McILLREE, N.W.M.P.
PIERRE LEVAILLER, his mark
ISADORE DUMOND, his mark
JEAN DUMOND, his mark
PETER HOURIE
F. GINGRAS
J. B. MITCHELL, Staff Constable, N.W.M.P.
E. H. PRICE, Hospital Steward, N.W.M.P.
XAVIER LETANGER, his mark
WILLIAM SINCLAIR
A. R. KENNEDY

R. I. Pritchard
L. Clark
W. McKay
W. D. Jarvis, Inspector, N.W.M.P.

Signed by the Chiefs and head men of the Willow Indians near Fort Carlton this 28th day of August, A.D. 1876, the same having been first read and explained by the Honourable James McKay, and Peter Erasmus, in the presence of the undersigned witnesses:

Chief
Wah-wee-kah-nick-kah-oo-tah-mah-hote, his mark
(or Neeh-cha-aw-asis)

Councillors
See-see-quan-ish, his mark,
Wee-tee-koo-wee-kah-maw-co, his mark

Joint Chiefs of the Willow Indians
Kah-mee-gis-too-way-sit, his mark
Kah-pay-yak-wahsk-oo-num, his mark
See-see-kwahn-is, his mark

Councillors of the Willow Indians
Kah-nah-lah-skow-waht, his mark
Kah-ah-tee-koo-wen, his mark
Kah-nah-mah-chew, his mark
Moon-ed-yahs, his mark
Oo-min-ah-kaw, his mark
Oo-tuk-koo-pah-kah-may-tow-may-yet, his mark

Witnesses
A. G. Jackes, M.D.
Joseph Genton
John A. Kerr

Pierre Levailler
W. D. Jarvis, N.W.M.P.

Signed by Her Majesty's Commissioners, and by the Chiefs and Headmen hereafter subscribing hereto, the same having been first read and explained to the Indians by the Honourable James McKay and Peter Erasmus, near Fort Pitt, this 9th day of September, A.D. 1876, in the presence of the undersigned witnesses:

Alexander Morris, L.G., N.W.T.

Indian Commissioners
James McKay
W. J. Christie

Cree Chiefs
Wee-kas-koo-khe-pay-yin, his mark.
Pee-yas-ee-wah-kah-we-chah-koot, his mark
James Seenum, his mark
Oo-nah-lat-mee-nah-hoos, his mark
See-kahs-kootch, his mark
Tus-tusk-ee-skwais, his mark
Pee-way-sis, his mark
Kee-ye-win, his mark

Chipewayan Chief
Kin-oo-say-oo, his mark.

Councillors to Wee-kas-koo-pay-yin
See-was-kwan, his mark
Wah-way-see-hoo-we-yin, his mark

Councillors to Pee-yas-ee-wah-kah-we-chah-koot
Tip-ee-skow-ah-chak, his mark
Pay-pay-see-see-moo, his mark

Councillors to See-kahs-kootch
Oo-now-uk-ee-pah-chas, his mark
My-now-way-sees, his mark

Councillors to Tus-tusk-ee-skwais
Oos-pwah-khun-is, his mark
Nee-ye-pee-tay-as-ee-kay-se, his mark

Councillors to Pee-way-sis
Mah-chah-mee-wis, his mark
Isaac Cardinal, his mark

Councillor to Kin-oo-say-oo
Antoine Xavier, his mark

Councillor to James Seenum
William Bull, his mark

Councillor to See-kahs-kootch
Wah-key-see-koot, his mark

Councillors to Kee-ye-win
Charles Cardinal, his mark
Pierre Wahbiskaw, his mark

Councillors to Wee-kas-koo-kee-pay-yin
Ki-yas-ee-kun, his mark
Kah-kee-oo-pah-tow, his mark

Councillor to Oo-nah-lat-mee-nah-hoos
Cake-cake, his mark

Councillor to James Seenum
Kam-oo-nin, his mark

Councillor to See-kahs-kootch
AH-SIS, his mark

Witnesses
A. G. JACKES, M.D.
JAS. McLEOD, Commissioner, N.W.M.P.
JAS. F. WALKER, Inspector, N.W.M.P.
+VITAL J., Bishop, St. Albert, O.M.I.
E. DALRYMPLE CLARKE, Adjutant., N.W.M.P.
CONSTANTINE SCOLLEN, Priest, O.M.I.
JOHN McDOUGALL, Methodist missionary
JOHN McELVEY
W. E. JONES
PETER C. PAMBRON
A. R. KENNEDY
PETER ERASMUS
THOMAS McKAY
JAMES SIMPSON
ELIZA HARDISTY
MARY McKAY

Recorded 24th February, 1877.
Lib. 27, Fol. 352.
L. A. CATELLIER,
Deputy Registrar-General of Canada.

Adhesion by Cree Indians

WE THE UNDERSIGNED Chiefs and Headmen, on behalf of ourselves and the other members of the Wood Cree Tribe of Indians, having had explained to us the terms of the treaty made and concluded near Carlton, on the 23rd day of August and on 28th day of said month respectively, and near Fort Pitt on the 9th day of September, 1876, between Her Majesty the Queen, by the Commissioners duly appointed to negotiate the said treaty, and the Plain and Wood Cree and other Tribes of Indians inhabiting the country within the limits defined in said treaty, but not having been present at the councils at which the articles of the said treaty were agreed upon, do now hereby for ourselves and the Bands which we represent, in consideration of the provisions of the said treaty being extended to us and the Bands which we represent, transfer, surrender, and relinquish to Her Majesty the Queen, Her heirs and successors, to and for the use of the Government of the Dominion of Canada, all our right, title and interest whatsoever which we and the said Bands which we represent hold and enjoy, or have held and enjoyed, of, in and to the territory included within the following limits: All and singular that portion or tract of land being the north part of the Land District of Prince Albert, as shown on the maps published by the Honourable the Minister of the Interior, dated at Ottawa on the 31st day of August, 1885; the same tract being north of the northerly limit of Treaty No. 6, North-West Territory, containing 11,066 square miles, be the same more or less, and more particularly described as follows: Commencing at a point being the north-west corner of projected Township No. 70, Range 10, west of the Third Initial Meridian; thence easterly along the northern boundaries of projected Townships Nos. 70 to the north-east corner of projected Township No. 70, Range 13, west of the Second Initial Meridian; thence southerly following the east boundary of said 13th Range of projected Townships to the northern limits of Treaty No. 6. into the projected Township No. 60; thence westerly following the northerly limit of Treaty No. 6 to the south-eastern shore of Green Lake, being at the north-easterly part of projected Township No. 58, Range 10, west of the Third Initial Meridian; thence following the westerly shore of Green Lake to the main inlet thereof known as Beaver River; thence up the right bank of Beaver River to its intersection with the west boundary of projected Township No. 62, Range 10, west of the Third Initial Meridian; thence northerly following the west boundary of projected townships of Range 10, west of the Third Initial Meridian, to the point of commencement.

Also, all our right, title and interest whatsoever to all other lands wherever situated, whether within the limits of any other treaty heretofore made, or hereafter to be made with Indians, and whether the said lands are situated in the North-West Territories or elsewhere in Her Majesty's Dominion, to have and to hold the same unto and for the use of Her Majesty the Queen, Her heirs and successors forever.

And we hereby agree to accept the several benefits, payments and reserves promised to the Indians adhering to the said treaty at Fort Pitt or Carlton; with the proviso as regards the amount to be expended annually for ammunition and twine, and as respects the amount to be expended for three years annually in provisions for the use of such Indians as are settled on reserves and are engaged in cultivating the soil, to assist them in such cultivation, that the expenditure on both of these items shall bear the same proportion to the number of Indians now treated with as the amounts for those two items as mentioned in Treaty No. 6 bore to the number of

Indians then treated with. And we solemnly engage to abide by, carry out and fulfil all the stipulations, obligations and conditions therein contained on the part of the Chiefs and Indians therein named to be observed and performed, and we agree in all things to conform to the articles of the said treaty, as if we ourselves and the Bands which we represent had been originally contracting parties thereto and had been present at the council held near Fort Pitt or near Carlton and had there attached our signatures to the said treaty.

IN WITNESS WHEREOF, Her Majesty's special Commissioners and the Chiefs and Councillors of the Bands hereby giving their adhesion to the said treaty have hereunto subscribed and set their hands at Montreal Lake this eleventh day of February, in the year of Our Lord one thousand eight hundred and eighty-nine.

Chiefs
JAMES ROBERTS
WILLIAM CHARLES, his mark

Councillors of James Roberts Band
AMOS CHARLES, his mark
JOSEPH CHARLES, his mark
ELIAS ROBERTS, his mark
JOHN COOK, his mark

Councillors of William Charles Band
Benjamin Bird, his mark
Isaac Bird, his mark
Patrick Bird, his mark
Moses Bird, his mark

Signed by the parties hereto in the presence of the undersigned witnesses, the same having been first explained to the Indians by the Venerable Archdeacon Mackay:

A. G. Irvine, Lt.-Colonel, Commissioner

R. Goulet, Commissioner

A. J. McNeill, Indian Department

H. J. Moberly, C.F., H.B.Co.

H. H. Alexander, Sgt., N.W.M.P.

C. V. Alloway

J. A. Mackay, Archdeacon of Saskatchewan

NOTES

1   Rena Dennison, "Herron's Whisper." www.pbs4549.org/onestate/herroncg.htm. See also Jeffrey Goodman, *American Genesis* (New York: Summit, 1981); and Vine Deloria, Jr., *Red Earth, White Lies: Native Americans and the Myth of Scientific Fact* (Golden, CO: Fulcrum, 1997). A scholarly review of *American Genesis* can be found at www.nativehistory.tripod.com/id15.html; see also www.native-languages.org/bering.htm.

2   *Delgamuukw* v. *British Columbia* [1991], CanLII 2372 (BC S.C.) (1991), 79 D.L.R. (4th) 185; [1991] 3 W.W.R. 97; [1991] 5 C.N.L.R. 5; Thomas Hobbes, *The Leviathan* (London: 1651), chap. XIII, "Of the Natural Condition of Mankind as Concerning their Felicity and Misery."

3   Kytwayhat is from the Makwa Sahgaiehcan First Nation, Treaty No. 6, near Loon Lake, Sask.

4   Virgil J. Vogel, *American Indian Medicine* (Norman, Okla.: University of Oklahoma Press, 1970), p. 159.

5   Quoted in Cornelius J. Jaenen, *Friend and Foe: Aspects of French-Amerindian Cultural Contact in the Sixteenth and Seventeenth Centuries* (Toronto: McClelland and Stewart, 1976).

6   Quoted in R. Obomsawin, "Traditional Indian Health and Nutrition: Forgotten Keys to Survival into the 21st Century," in Thomas Berger (Commissioner), *Selected Readings in Support of Indian and Inuit Health Consultation*, Vol. II (Ottawa: Health and Welfare, 1980), p. 44.

7   Edward Everett Hale (1822-1909), *The Life of Christopher Columbus: From His own Letters and Journals and other Documents of His Time*. University of Virginia Library, Electronic Text Center. http://etext.lib.virginia.edu/toc/modeng/public/HalLife.html.

8   *Johnson and Grahams Lease* v. *M'Intosh* (21 U.S. (8 Wheat.) 543 (1823); *Cherokee Nation* v. *Georgia* (30 U.S. (5 Pet.) 1 (1831); *Worcester* v. *Georgia* (31 U.S. (6 Pet.) 515 (1832).

9   "Letter of Columbus, Describing the Results of His First Voyage," in Cecil Jane (ed. and trans.), *The Four Voyages of Columbus*, Vol. 1 (New York: Dover Publications, 1988).

10 John Bostock and H. T. Riley (eds.), *Pliny the Elder, The Natural History* (London: Taylor and Francis, 1855). www.perseus.tufts.edu/cgi-bin/ptext.

11 *Haida Nation* v. *British Columbia (Minister of Forests)*, [2004] 3 S.C.R. 511, 204 S.C.C. 73, para. 25.

12 Alexander Morris, *The Treaties of Canada with the Indians of Manitoba and the North-West Territories, including the Negotiations on which they were based* (Saskatoon: Fifth House, 1991; Toronto: Belford, Clarke, 1880), p. 215.

13 See Paul A. Chartrand (ed.), *Who Are Canada's Aboriginal People? Recognition, Definition, and Jurisdiction* (Saskatoon: Purich Publishing, 2002), p.107: "The idea of derivative rights recalls the notion behind the doctrine of *terra nullius*, which denies the existence of Indigenous people, in the sense that they do not legally matter when Europeans arrive, and who therefore have no history that matters."

14 International Court of Justice, Advisory Opinion regarding Western Sahara, Oct. 16, 1975.

15 *Mabo and Others* v. *Queensland* (No. 2) [1992] 5 C.N.L.R. 1, 107 A.L.R. 1.

16 Duncan Scott, "Indian Affairs, 1763-1841," in Adam Shortt and Arthur Doughty (eds.), *Canada and Its Provinces,* Vol. IV (Toronto: Glasgow, Brook and Company, 1914), pp. 695-725.

17 *Haida Nation* v. *British Columbia (Minister of Forests)* [2004], 3 S.C.R. 511; *Mikisew Cree First Nation* v. *Canada (Minister of Canadian Heritage)* [2005], 3 S.C.R. 388; *Delgamuukw* v. *British Columbia* [1997], 3 S.C.R. 1010; 5. *Taku River Tlingit First Nation* v. *British Columbia (Project Assessment Director)* [2004], 3 S.C.R. 550; *R.* v. *Badger,* [1996] 1 S.C.R. 771; *R.* v. *Sparrow,* [1990] 1 S.C.R. 1075; *R.* v. *Van der Peet,* [1996] 2 S.C.R. 507; *R.* v. *Sioui,* [1990] 1 S.C.R. 1025; *British Columbia (Minister of Forests)* v. *Okanagan Indian Band* [2003], 3 S.C.R. 371; *R.* v. *Gladue,* [1999] 1 S.C.R. 688.

18 Morris, *The Treaties of Canada*, p. 168.

19 Treaty No. 8 was signed by six leaders of Canadian First Nations and the British Crown at Lesser Slave Lake, Alberta in June 1899. It covered 39 First Nations communities, and it was here that Morris said its terms were to have effect "as long as the sun shines, the grass grows and the river flows." www.atns.net.au/biogs/A001792b.htm

20 Morris, *The Treaties of Canada*, p. 204.

21 *Ibid.*, p. 213.

22 J. H. Baker, *An Introduction to English Legal History*, Third Edition (Dublin: Butterworth's, 1990), pp 266.

23 *Ibid.*

24 Stat. 59 Geo. III, c.46.

25 Baker, *An Introduction to English Legal History*, p. 87, note 10.

26 *Johnson and Grahams Lease* v. *M'Intosh* (1823) 8 Wheaton 543.

27 Morris, *The Treaties of Canada*, p. 231.

28 *Ibid.*, p. 239.

29 See Appendix A, para. 3.

30 *R.* v. *Jacob*, 2002 YKTC 15 at para. 134.

31 Morris, *The Treaties of Canada*, p. 211.

32 *Ibid.*, p. 212.

33 *Ibid.*, p. 193.

34 *Ibid.*, pp. 212-213.

35 The Robinson Huron Treaty, Sept. 9, 1850, at Sault Ste. Marie.

36 *The Constitution Act, 1867* (U.K.), 30 & 31 Victoria, c. 3. At s. 91 (24).

37 *A.-G. Can.* v. *A.-G. Ont. A.-G. Que.* v. *A.-G. Ont.* [1897], A.C. 199 at p. 213 (also reported: (1896) C.R. [11] A.C. 308). http://library.usask.ca/native/cnlc/vol03/483.html.)

38 *R.* v. *Sikyea* (1964), 43 D.L.R. (2d) 150 (also reported: [1964] 2 C.C.C. 325, 46 W.W.R. 65, 43 C.R. 83), p. 213. http://library.usask.ca/native/cnlc/vol06/583.html.)

39 *Simon* v. *The Queen* [1985], 2 S.C.R. 387, 1985 CanLII 11 (S.C.C.) Under s. 88 of the *Indian Act*, when the terms of a treaty come into conflict with federal legislation, the latter prevails, subject to whatever may be the effect of s. 35 of the *Constitution Act, 1982*. It has been held to be within the exclusive power of Parliament under s. 91(24) of the *Constitution Act, 1867*, to derogate from rights recognized in a treaty agreement made with the Indians. See *R.* v. *Sikyea* (1964), 43 D.L.R. (2d) 150.

40 Albert Memmi, *The Colonizer and the Colonized* (Boston: Beacon Press, 1991).

41 J. M. Blaut, *The Colonizer's Model of the World: Geographical Diffusion and Eurocentric History* (New York: The Guilford Press, 1993).

42 Marie Battiste and James (Sákéj) Youngblood Henderson, *Protecting Indigenous Knowledge and Heritage: A Global Challenge* (Saskatoon: Purich Publishing, 2000).

43 *Indian Act*, R.S.C. 1985 c. I-5 s. 6.

44 Richard Tuck, *Natural Rights Theories: Their Origin and Development* (Cambridge: Cambridge University Press, 1979).

45 In 1532, de Victoria delivered two lectures: *De Indes Noviter Inventis* (On the Indians Lately Discovered) and *De Jure Belli Hispanorum in Barbaros* (On the Law of War Made by the Spaniards on the Barbarians). Both appear in Ernest Nys (ed.) and John Pawley Bate (trans.), *De Indis et de Jure Belli Relectiones*, Classics of International Law, #7, Bk. 1 (Washington, DC: Carnegie Institution of Washington, DC, 1917), p. 83.

46 Antony Anghie, *Imperialism, Sovereignty and the Making of International Law* (Cambridge: Cambridge University Press, 2004).

47 John Locke, *Two Treatises of Government* (Peter Laslett, ed.), (Cambridge: Cambridge University Press, 1960).

48 *Ibid.*, pp. 278-79.

49 *Ibid.*, p. 294.

50 *R.* v. *Badger* [1996], 2 C.N.L.R. 77 (S.C.C.).

51 *Indian Act*, R.S.C. 1985 c. I-5 s.6.

52 *The Hunting and Fishing Heritage Act*, S.B.C. 2002 c-79, *Heritage Hunting and Fishing Act*, S.O.2002 c.-10.

ABOUT THE AUTHOR

Harold Johnson — husband, father, grandfather, brother, and uncle — lives and writes from a log cabin in Northern Saskatchewan without the impediments of electricity and running water. His Swedish father, trapper, fisherman, died when Harold was eight years old. His Cree Mother taught him his bush skills. One spring while she and twelve-year-old Harold were walking the trapline, she told him, "You have to learn these ways, how to set traps, how to set a fish net. You have to learn how to make your living off the land, just in case anything ever happens to that other world, so you can survive."

At the age of 17 Harold joined the Canadian Navy. Later he worked as an itinerant across western and northern Canada. He has been a miner, a logger, a mechanic, a labourer, and a heavy equipment operator. In 1991 Harold quit the Key Lake Uranium Mine to attend university. He graduated with a bachelor's degree in law from the University of Saskatchewan in 1995, and with a master's degree in law from Harvard University in 1996.

Harold survives in both worlds — from an internship with the International Labour Office in Geneva, Switzerland, to presently working with his wife Joan in a private practice law office in La Ronge, Saskatchewan. He balances this world with the operation of his family's traditional trapline using a dog team, and he belongs to the Northland Fishermen's Co-operative that his father helped start in 1955.